ARCHERY

GOODYEAR
Physical Activities Series

Edited by J. Tillman Hall

Archery	Jean A. Barrett *California State College* *at Fullerton*
Badminton	James Poole *Tulane University*
Bowling	Norman E. Showers *Southern Illinois University*
Fencing	Nancy L. Curry *Southwest Missouri State College*
Folk Dance	J. Tillman Hall *University of Southern California*
Golf	Edward F. Chui *University of Hawaii*
Men's Basketball	Richard H. Perry *University of Southern California*
Soccer	John Callaghan *University of Southern California*
Social Dance	John G. Youmans *Temple University*
Swimming	Donald L. Gambril *California State College* *at Long Beach*
Tennis	Barry C. Pelton *University of Houston*

Fundamentals of Physical Education	J. Tillman Hall *University of Southern California* Kenneth C. Lersten *University of Southern California* Merril J. Melnick *University of Southern California* Talmage W. Morash *San Fernando Valley State College* Richard H. Perry *University of Southern California* Robert A. Pestolesi *California State College at Long Beach* Burton Seidler *California State College at Los Angeles*
Women's Basketball	Ann Stutts *San Fernando Valley State College*
Women's Gymnastics	Mary L. Schreiber *California State College at Los Angeles*

FORTHCOMING BOOKS

Handball	Rollin Wright *University of Illinois*
Men's Gymnastics	Gordon Maddux *California State College at Los Angeles*
Volleyball	Charles "Randy" Sandefur *California State College at Long Beach*

GOODYEAR PUBLISHING COMPANY
Pacific Palisades, California 90272

Goodyear Physical Activities Series

J. Tillman Hall: *Series Editor*

Jean A. Barrett

California State College at Fullerton

ARCHERY

Acknowledgments

I wish to extend sincere thanks to all those who helped in the preparation of the book. The assistance of Donna Bohannon, who posed for the pictures, and Janice Keasling, who prepared the illustrated material, is greatly appreciated. I am deeply indebted to Kay Malucky, who prepared the final manuscript and served as "devil's advocate" throughout its development. To Maureen C. Rams, who rekindled my interest in archery, a very special thank you. The contributions of the many students in my archery classes cannot go without mention. Contact with each individual has promoted better understanding of the learning process and forced me to delve deeper into the significance of archery as a sport.

ARCHERY
Jean A. Barrett

© Copyright 1969 by
GOODYEAR PUBLISHING COMPANY
Pacific Palisades, California

Library of Congress Catalog Card Number: 69-17985

Current printing (last number):

10 9 8 7 6 5 4 3 2 1

Printed in the United States of America

Contents

Editor's note

The Goodyear Publishing Company presents a series of physical education books written by instructors expert in their respective fields.

These books on major sports are intended as supplementary material for the instructor and to aid the student in the understanding and mastery of the sport of his choice. Each book covers its fundamentals—the beginning techniques, rules and customs, equipment and terms—and gives to the reader the spirit of the sport.

Each author of this series brings to the reader the knowledge and skill he has acquired over many years of teaching and coaching. We sincerely hope that these books will prove invaluable to the college student or any student of the sport.

In ARCHERY, Jean Barrett describes the techniques and analyzes the fundamentals a student must master in order to become an accomplished archer. From the experience of her teaching at California State College in Fullerton, Jean Barrett brings the student a book that contains a comprehensive analysis of the fundamental techniques such as stringing the bow, inserting the arrow, aiming, and releasing the arrow. Also, suggested tasks for the student are included in each chapter, along with great emphasis on safety.

The numerous tables indicate possible difficulties and suggested solutions will be of interest to any archer. Even though target archery is stressed, a variety of sports and games, such as clout shooting, flight shooting, hunting, and archery golf add interest and new aspects of pleasure for the student of this ancient, though modern sport.

A Means to an End – An End in Itself

Modern technology has eliminated the utilitarian reasons for developing proficiency with the bow and arrow. The bow, originally used as a weapon for defense or conquest or as a means of securing food, is in present day society a recreational sport activity. To be sure, basic needs still exist in some primitive cultures that are fulfilled through use of the bow.

DEVELOPMENT AS A SPORT

Precisely how and when the bow originated is not known, but it certainly was one of the earliest weapons of man. The bow has been a part of recorded history for more than 50,000 years, but its existence was established well before that time. Archeologists estimate from cave drawings depicting archers that the bow was in use at least 100,000 years ago. For thousands of years, human beings used propelled arrows to protect themselves from wild animals. At the same time, archery skill was used to obtain food. The bow became a symbol of strength and power; it gave man a certain status and advantage in his environment.

Over the centuries archery gained significance in man's life. The bow and arrow became associated with all of his activities and endeavors, all of his moods and emotions. The bow was a weapon of survival, a tool that established man's superiority over animals. With it, direct physical contact with a foe was no longer necessary.

Man's love of music was stimulated by the twang of the bow string. The harp was developed by adding strings to the bow and archery became further entwined with the culture. In Greek legend, the Amazons demonstrated the ability of women to use the bow as a weapon; they made the bow a weapon of conquest. On the mainland of Greece, the beautifully designed Greek bow became a different symbol, associated with Diana and the hunt and Cupid and love.

With the exception of some Australian tribes, the bow was known to all primitive people throughout the Eastern world. War weapons such as slings and spears became outmoded as the bow and arrow was perfected. According to the Bible, the Israelites and the Egyptians were accomplished archers. The significance of the bow and arrow as a weapon of war can be attested by accounts of world-changing battles. Bows were developed to suit the needs of horsemen as well as foot soldiers. Orientals designed a short bow especially for use on horseback. The English were noted for the use of the long-type bow, while the French adopted and perfected the crossbow. The battles of Hastings, Crecy, Agincourt and then the War of the Roses were military engagements of historical importance in which the bow played a significant part.

The Greeks and Turks are given credit for the development of the first composite bows, made of wood, bone, and leather strips. It is interesting to note that it wasn't until 1959 that modern flight shooters broke the distance record credited to an ancient bow. The remarkable Turks were able to cast arrows eight hundred yards with a complex reflex bow that assumed a "C" shape when unstrung. This was quite an accomplishment for the ancients, when you consider they lacked the technical and material advantages of our modern bowyers.

When gunpowder was developed, the value of the bow as a weapon for war or survival began steadily to decline. Firearms eliminated the need to spend many hours becoming proficient in accurately discharging an arrow. Henry VIII, an avid English archer who also enjoyed wagering, is credited with the development of archery as a competitive sport. Archery societies or clubs were established in England over 350 years ago. The Toxophilite Society, The Richmond Archers, The Royal Edinborough Archers, and The Finsbury Archers are some of the earliest clubs devoted to shooting.

The American Indians' skill and daring with the bow is part of our own national history. The earliest known archery club in the United States was the United Bowman of Philadelphia. Founded in 1828, this organization is still active today. The National Archery Association (NAA) was formed in in 1879, but it was not until 1940 that an association for field archery was organized. At first, field archery tournaments were restricted to instinctive or bare-bow shooters and attracted many people who enjoyed shooting under conditions that closely represent those of hunting. Today field competition is conducted in two divisions, instinctive (bare bow) and freestyle (sight).

During the first quarter of the twentieth century, interest in bow hunting was stimulated when Dr. S. Pope shot seventeen African lions with a long bow. Today, hunters try for all types of game from birds to the grizzly bear. Popularity of bow hunting has caused many states to enact special laws and provide bow seasons in addition to the regular gun hunting seasons.

Archery is scheduled to become a gold medal sport in the 1972 Olympic games. The XIX Olympiad held in Mexico City in the fall of 1968 allowed archery to be listed as an unofficial or demonstration sport for the first time. It seems paradoxical that one of the world's oldest sport forms has only recently been accepted as an Olympic sport. There has been much controversy over what constitutes amateur standing in archery. Many present competitions are of the open variety, where amateurs and professionals shoot at the same time. In addition, some prizes in strictly amateur meets have exceeded the value limit acceptable to the Olympic Committee. Our potential Olympic archers are today's young people. Unlike many sports skills, it is quite possible to develop a high degree of archery proficiency in a relatively short time. Proper practice, great desire and interest, as well as ability are the ingredients needed to turn a fair performer into a champion.

Many colleges have varsity archery teams for both men and women. The National Collegiate Archery Coaches Association governs meets between colleges and also sponsors the National Collegiate Archery Championships. An increasing number of recreation departments are including archery facilities in their planning. The number of participants in all forms of shooting has increased from 1.7 million in 1946 to over 4.7 million in 1960, with interest continually growing. Archery has come of age as a modern sport form.

SOMETHING OF VALUE

The Puritan ethic, so influential in the development of early American culture, remains with us to some extent today. In our early history, work was considered sacred; play was the reward that could be enjoyed only as a result of much productive effort. The idea of engaging in activity just for pleasure is still a little hard for some people to swallow. To think of sport and play as truly educational and enlarging experiences that help us to understand man as a human entity seems to be beyond the comprehension of many individuals.

Today's college student is more than preoccupied with the task of finding meaning in life: he is vitally concerned with who he is and with what he does. He is concerned with individual freedom and individual integrity. He thoughtfully, and sometimes forcefully, questions the significance of existing values. In short, the student is engaged in a vigorous and dedicated search for basic meanings in life. It is sometimes difficult to see how participation in skilled activity, such as archery, relates to the goals of education or to the individual search for meaning in life. Perhaps clues to the potential for human development and individual growth can be found in the discussion which follows.

Archery Is For Everyone

Archery is a pleasurable activity! The various forms of the sport hold appeal for a wide variety of people. Participants are not limited by age or need be severely restricted because of physical handicaps. Boys, girls, men, and women have opportunities to participate on equal bases. Archery is an individual sport. No one else need be present to enjoy the activity. Archery is a family recreational pastime. It is relatively inexpensive and can be enjoyed year around, indoors and outdoors. Archery is a club sport. Clubs provide occasions to meet people, to engage in competition on a formal or informal basis, to work for common goals, and to share interests and experiences. But most of all—archery is a fun activity!

Physical Benefits

The ordinary physiological effects of exercise can be realized to a certain degree through archery. There is a good deal of walking and bending of a type that differs from ordinary work activity. Drawing the bow and holding the anchor position helps to build strength and endurance in shoulder and upper back muscles. Contraction of the abdominals adds strength necessary for maintenance of erect posture. Expansion or stretching of the chest muscles helps to offset fatigue that builds up after sitting for long periods of time—an occupational hazard for college students. Archery helps establish muscular balance and serves to counteract some of the effects of a sedentary way of life.

Emotional Values

Man is a complex creature with many needs and desires. The technological revolution, producing constant changes in man's way of life, adds to the stress and anxiety. Man, in a sense, is a victim of his own intellectual ingenuity. Automation, computers, and assembly lines eliminate many of the former opportunities for personal satisfaction. Pressures and tensions seem to mount to almost unbearable proportions.

Man's image of himself as a useful human being is daily being chipped away. Man used to take pride in his work. His ability to start something and see it through to completion gave him a sense of achievement. Work was personally satisfying; it built his self confidence and gave a feeling of control over destiny. Considering our Puritan heritage, it is almost paradoxical that, today, these basic human needs are more readily met through participation in sport and recreational activities.

The ability to handle a bow and arrow competently is personally gratifying; it gives one a sense of pride in one's own abilities and serves to build self-esteem and self-confidence. There is a great deal of satisfaction in sending an arrow exactly where it is aimed. This feeling of accomplishment is enhanced by the knowledge that the work involved in disciplining the mind and body helps one gain control physically and over one's will.

All people need socially acceptable outlets for aggressive drives and creative impulses. Feelings of anger and hate are usually denied open expression in a civilized society. Acceptable ways of "letting off steam" must be found. Sport activity provides one such avenue. Anger and frustration seem to dissipate as arrows are sent winging toward an objective. Concentration, so necessary for skilled performance in archery, serves to melt anxiety into meaninglessness. Involvement provides a means of escape, a chance to "get away from it all." Cares and concerns of the day-to-day world are seen in clearer perspective and better objectivity once some of the tension is released.

The rules of sport serve to free the individual. They provide the performer with a less complex, well-defined world where all energies can be directed toward the accomplishment of a goal of one's own choosing. In the context of sport, man has a chance to experience himself as a human being.

On Sport and Play

Spontaneous activity of a joyful nature, which has no particular goal as its end, is characteristic of play activity. Play, as opposed to sport, can be broadly defined as carefree, joyful activity, pursued purely in a non-serious manner. The length of time, size, or extent of the play area, number of participants and the like, are subject to change by whim or convenience. Sport, on the other hand, is governed by an elaborate set of rules that define the equipment to be used, the number of performers, the area for conducting the activity, the time period, the method of scoring, and, often, the expected conduct of the participant himself. Sport operates upon a basis of law and order; it could not survive on a basis of expediency.

There are many forms of archery and each can be pursued as a recreational activity or, in the truest meaning of that word, as sport. The degree of personal involvement, circumstances of participation, and purpose of the activity are factors determining the character of the experience. The potential for understanding one's own nature and the nature of others is present when one becomes involved in archery.

Participation in any sport indicates a willingness to accept the code governing the activity. The performer voluntarily assumes particular responsibilities for his own behavior and makes certain moral and ethical commitments. Basic emotional and personality patterns are brought into sharper focus by behavior in competitive situations.

Sport demands that each individual put forth a sincere effort to produce the best performance of which he is capable. This is a moral commitment. Ability or inability to produce an honest attempt provides insight into the nature of the individual's value system and his character. Archery is not an easy sport to master since there are so many opportunities for human error. Shooting is a challenge that provides an opportunity to explore the depth of commitment to a desired goal. The quantitative score expresses how precisely the archer has focussed his materials and abilities, while the manner in which he deals with success or failure presents him with a startlingly clear picture of himself. The rules of sport leave no room for pretense. Alibies or excuses unveil an image of the self that may be more-than-expected or less-than-desired. Fortitude, courage, and persistence in developing one's shooting ability may introduce a more desirable self-image.

SUGGESTED TASKS FOR THE STUDENT

1. Locate and list significant examples of the use of the bow from literature, art and history.
2. Write a short statement of what kind of a person you think you are. What do you think your values are?
3. Try and recall some situation that presented a challenge or a threat to you. Write a statement of how you reacted in the situation and explore the complications for you as an individual.
4. List all of the experiences you can recall that made you feel like a more worthwhile individual.
5. Indicate in writing, your evaluation of your ability to learn to perform in a skillful manner.

Face Up – Sight In

2

Barring some serious physical handicap or neurological disorder, just about everyone can learn to shoot a bow and arrow proficiently. Many students feel that they are not "good athletes," that they do not possess the qualities associated with good skill performance. If this is the case, the first step toward a mediocre performance has been taken. In effect, a barrier has been erected serving to restrict learning and skill development.

There is a great deal of available information concerned with the acquisition of motor skills. The specialist in the area of motor performance attempts to apply motor-learning principles to the teaching-learning situation. Unfortunately, the average student is usually oblivious to many of the factors that influence his learning and skill development, often clinging to misconceptions that impede his progress. This chapter deals with some general considerations associated with motor learning and their application to development of archery skills. The material included is not a complete summary of the information available but rather a sketch of present knowledge based on scientific evidence. The points discussed were chosen because of their particular relevance to learning archery skills. It is felt that if the student is better informed about the nature of learning, he will have a better understanding of his potential for success.

NATURE OF THE LEARNER

Man is an intelligent, physical, social-emotional being endowed with certain common characteristics of his species. At the same time, he is different from others of his kind in that these traits vary, to a greater or lesser degree, for each individual. Attainment of skill appears to be related to a number of factors. Because the individual is totally involved in any learning experience, certain personal factors are important considerations.

Sex, Build and Strength

Sex, body build, body type, and strength may influence achievement in some sport skills while not in others. Physiological and anatomical differences between the sexes are particularly relevant in skill acquisition when strength and power are factors. However, many women fail to develop skill to their fullest potential because they assume they are incapable of a high level of performance due to structural and functional differences. Variations in the attainment level of the female can often be caused by other things such as lack of social acceptance of women participants in many sport activities and individual motivational level. Sex differences are of little significance in attaining proficiency in archery skills with the possible exception of some forms, such as hunting and fishing. Archery is a socially acceptable sport form which can be mastered and enjoyed equally by both sexes, young and old alike.

Body build or body type contributes to success in some motor activities. Height and weight, however, appear to have little value in predicting achievement. Potential for performance in archery is not directly related to body proportions, but variables in length of limbs are determinants in selection of equipment and do affect distance and aim to some extent. (See Chapter 5.)

Insufficient strength in certain body areas important to a particular movement can be a deterrent to learning and performance. The archer must have adequate strength in many muscles used in the movement if he is to perform well. If this strength is not present, learning will be delayed or inhibited. The individual must possess enough muscle power to draw the bow with ease and comfort to avoid introducing errors into his performance. The following exercises and activities are helpful in building strength in the muscle groups used in the shooting act and in stretching appropriate body areas.

1. Push ups. Women should use the modified push ups; men, the regular type.
2. Shoulders stretchers or arm flings. Start with arms extended out to side; bring arms forward so that they cross in front of body; fling or force arms back. This will stretch chest muscles and help tighten back muscles.
3. Lifting light weights. Start with side stride position and bend over at the waist, arms extended. Keeping arms straight, lift light weights by moving the arms sideways to shoulder height. Weights used should become progressively heavier as strength is developed.
4. Toe or floor touches. Hold both feet together and bend over at waist, touching fingertips to floor or toes. The exercise helps to stretch leg tendons and back muscles.
5. Simulated draw and hold. Stand with feet comfortably apart. Raise arms so that hands are close to intended anchor position. The bow hand is turned palm out with the fingers in a bent position; the fingers of the string hand are hooked into the fingers of the other hand. Pull as if the elbows were being forced back and the action of the shoulder, back, and upper arm muscles can be felt.
6. Fingers and arm. (1) Squeeze a small rubber ball with fingers. (2) Start with hand placed palm down on a

table. Apply pressure and roll up on fingertips keeping second and third finger joints straight.

Physical Abilities

Research in the area of motor learning has led to the generalization that skill development is specific for each individual. Factors such as coordination, timing, movement speed, balance, acuity of senses, and kinesthetic sense (feeling) are important in producing a skillful performance, but each of these abilities must be developed for a particular activity. A person who is accomplished in one sport area will not necessarily demonstrate similar competency in other sports. Successful performance in motor tasks depends on a number of things. Prior experience and practice in a wide variety of physical activities, however, may be an aid in learning to perform well. The more experienced and exercised individual may be able to interpret information relative to his performance more quickly than a person who has had limited participation in sports.

Information about body position, distance, direction, force, etc., is constantly being fed to the individual through his senses. So much information is available that the performer must be able to select that which is relevant to the task and disregard those things which are irrelevant. We generally refer to this as "the power of concentration." Awareness of what is important and the capacity to organize and interpret sensory and perceptual information promotes appropriate motor activity. Ability to focus on the task at hand and obliviousness to the inappropriate stimuli present is important in archery. Shooting experience and extensive practice in the actual situation are helpful in this respect. Unnecessary distractions, such as tight clothing and inappropriate footwear, should be avoided. Since speed of movement is not essential to target shooting, the ability to inhibit movement until the proper moment is a more important consideration.

Social-Emotional Factors

Each person brings his own set of attitudes, values, and needs to the learning situation. How a person feels about himself and the activity he is engaged in will influence his learning. Emotional status, motivation, and level of inspiration are among the factors that explain variations in performance.

Whether tension, stress, and anxiety help or hinder performance depends on the individual and the situation. However, a very high anxiety level or an extremely stressful situation usually hinders performance, particularly when the motor task is complex. Fear builds stress and anxiety and is often introduced into a situation by the performer who feels insecure about his own abilities.

If a learner is not motivated to execute the desired response, he will not learn. Knowledge of results is a form of reinforcement and helps to sustain individual effort. There is always some feedback available in motor skills, and higher levels of performance are reached if there is specific and immediate knowledge of results. Archery has this very important factor built in. The performer immediately knows whether he has hit or missed and forms a picture of his degree of error or accuracy. Quantitative scores provide continuing information about improvement and level of achievement.

The individual affects his own success by the personal goal he sets. If a reasonably lofty objective is envisioned and successfully accomplished, confidence is built and the individual's level of aspiration rises.

Competition

Some individuals feel that competition is not conducive to good performance; scientific literature indicates otherwise. Competition may not prove helpful in the initial learning stages, but performance appears to improve in a competitive atmosphere once the learner has developed some degree of proficiency. The anxiety and stress of a competitive situation for some people may be the factor detrimental to performance rather than the competitive situation itself.

NATURE OF THE TASK

Motor skills are generally classified as fine and gross, depending upon the amount of movement involved. Sport skills fall in the latter category. Gross motor tasks are further defined as discrete or continuous. A continuous skill involves a series of locomotor actions, each of which must occur in a particular order. Discrete tasks embody a single execution and archery can be placed in this classification. Length and type of practices and rate of skill acquisition are other factors that influence learning and performance in archery and should be kept in mind.

Complexity and Form

Shooting a bow and arrow is a relatively simple task in comparison with sport skills such as a tennis forehand drive. The tennis player must be able to judge the speed and distance of an oncoming projectile, position himself properly, and execute a series of movements to successfully return the ball. The archer, on the other hand, is aware of or estimates the distance to the target, which is usually stationary, and executes the act from a static position. He repeats exactly the same basic movements each time he shoots, adjusting only the elevation and lateral position of the bow arm to send his arrows in the intended direction.

The particular form a person uses in executing a skill is an individual matter and is really a way of expressing one's self. Good form is based on scientific and a priori evidence and should be developed. Individual differences, especially in body structure and proportions, may necessitate allowances for several means of execution, but the underlying mechanical and kinesiological principles are still evidenced. The principles related to good form in shooting are fully discussed in Chapter 5. The learner should strive to understand mechanical, anatomical, and kinesiological principles and how they apply.

Initially the basics should be practiced. Then, individual variations, either suggested by the instructor or discovered through experimentation, can be employed.

Learning Rate

The rate of skill acquisition varies with the individual and the particular skill. Early success does not necessarily indicate later achievement. Generally speaking, the initial phase of learning is usually quite rapid. Gradually, even as practice continues, progress slows down to a level of almost no improvement. However, performance and learning are not exactly the same. Learning can be occurring even though the performance does not show improvement in relation to the effort expended. The term "learning plateau" is often used to describe the phenomenon where the performance seems to reach a stalemate or even deteriorate somewhat. Motivation, failure to learn the skill properly, or inattention to the performance are elements that contribute to this slowdown. Effort should be made to analyze and correct the difficulty so that progress can continue. Each individual should allow enough time to perfect his own performance. Keep in mind the fact that the time needed will not be the same for each person. If a "plateau" is reached, the archer must have patience and allow motivation to continue to prevail. Remember, learning may still be taking place even though there is no appraciable improvement in performance. If there is a desire to improve, this intent will lead to better performance.

Practice

Practice may make perfect, but it is more correct to say that practice serves to make permanent. Errors in form or execution may actually be perpetuated if practiced. A number of factors must be taken into consideration if the practice period is to be beneficial. The learner must be aware of, and pay attention to, clues relevant to his performance.

Extended practice periods are valuable to those individuals who demonstrate initial difficulty with the task. Supervision and consistent evaluation aid in obtaining a reliable measure of the benefit of practice sessions. No single method of instruction or practice is appropriate for all skills or every student. Each learner must be able to ascertain his needs and direct his practice efforts accordingly. At first, it is better to learn the skill as an entity. If a particular aspect of the task appears to be hindering the performance, that part should be practiced so that the specific difficulty can be overcome.

Actual involvement in the setting where the skill is to be used is the best practice. However, picturing the task mentally, thinking through what is to be done, can aid in learning. Some people need more practice than others because of differences in learning rate. The student should recognize this and arrange sufficient time for practice outside the regular class period if he is to reap the benefits related to skillful participation in a sport activity.

MEANING FOR THE ARCHER

There is nothing like the feeling of accomplishment when the arrow strikes the "bull" or gold of the target. Conversely, continued frustration serves to lessen initiative and desire to perfect shooting skill. The learner can do much to contribute to his own success in archery by evaluating his own motivation, needs, desires, and applying his knowledge about learning motor skills to the particular situation. If a definite goal is kept in mind, there is nothing to stand in the way of reaching it—except the individual himself. The goals must be realistic and yet challenging, with sufficient time allotted for attainment.

The learner must do his own learning. No one can get inside his body and think through or perform an act for him. He alone is responsible for and capable of achieving success. Physical characteristics must be considered in determining form and selecting equipment but these do not necessarily affect the potential for performance. There is no such thing as general motor ability or the "all around athlete"; each person is capable of performing well, but some people require longer than others to successfully demonstrate an acceptable level of performance.

Level of aspiration, motivation, attitude, and need to achieve are individual variables which affect results. These factors are probably more important in learning archery than in other athletic endeavors. Adequate instruction and appropriate repetition and practice are necessary to learning, but the final measure of success or failure rests with the beginner himself.

People usually persist in a sport in which they feel they can become adept. The benefits derived from activity are consistent with the effort put forth and the manner in which the task is approached. Believe in yourself and your ability to learn. *FACE UP – SIGHT IN* on your target!

SUGGESTED TASKS FOR THE STUDENT

1. Determine your strength needs. Select a number of developmental exercises and write out a program for yourself that includes a time schedule. Keep a record so that you will be aware of your progress.
2. List your ideas about motor learning prior to reading this chapter as you recall them. Check your list with the information given in the book. Note the differences and similarities.
3. Make a list of the factors affecting performance, and analyze how you feel about yourself with regard to these points.
4. Set a definite goal for yourself. What is the *exact* score you desire to attain? Define your level of aspiration.
5. Set up a definite date to achieve the desired score or objective.
6. Develop a written plan for achieving your objective and put it into action. Keep in mind your self-analysis and the factors influencing learning.
7. Keep a record of your progress toward your goal. Record anecdotal notes of your feelings about yourself and your ability to perform after each day of shooting.
8. Try to recall what it felt like to hit the center of the gold for the very first time. How did it compare with other experiences you have had in other areas?

Pertinent Archery Terms

ADDRESSING THE TARGET   Standing ready for target shooting. The body is at right angles to the target with the feet straddling the shooting line.

ANCHOR   The position at which the string hand is fixed while holding and aiming.

ARCHERY   The art, skill, and practice of shooting with a bow and arrow.

ARCHERY GOLF   An adaptation of the game of golf, played on a real or simulated golf course, using a bow and arrow.

ARM GUARD   A device used to protect the bow arm from string abrasions.

ARROW REST   A projection on the bow handle upon which the arrow rests.

BACK   The side of the bow away from the string.

BACKING   Material put on the back of the bow to improve the cast or reinforce the bow.

BELLY   The side of the bow facing the string and nearest to the archer.

BLUNT   A hard rubber, metal, or plastic tip used for hunting small game.

BOW ARM OR BOW HAND   The hand or arm which holds the bow in preparation for and during shooting.

BOW RACK   A device, either portable or stationary, designed to hold the bow while it is not being used.

BOW SIGHT   A device, attached to the bow, which the archer uses when aiming.

BOWYER   One who makes bows.

BRACE   To string a bow; to prepare a bow for shooting by putting the string into the nock of the bow.

BRACER   An arm guard.

CAST   The speed with which an arrow leaves the bow; the distance a bow can shoot.

CLOUT   A target flat on the ground which usually measures 48' in diameter.

COCK FEATHER   The feather at right angles to the nock of the arrow. Usually a different color from the other two feathers.

COMPOSITE BOW   A bow consisting of different layers of materials.

CREEPING   The slightly forward movement of a fully drawn arrow before it is released.

CREST   The marking on the arrow, usually composed of one or more colors.

DEAD RELEASE   Allowing the fingers of the string hand to open gradually on the release, thus reducing some of the tension and cast.

DOUBLE ROUND   A round consisting of two identical single rounds.

DRAW   The process of bringing the string back into a position to release an arrow; the distance to which a bow is drawn.

DRIFT   A deviation of the arrow in flight due to the wind.

ELEVATION   The height of the bow hand when aiming.

END   Six arrows shot in succession or in two groups of three; in field archery, four arrows; in indoor archery, five arrows.

EYE   A loop in the end of the string fitted into the nock of the bow.

FACE   See "belly."

FIELD CAPTAIN   The presiding official over a men's shooting line or a mixed shooting line.

FINGER TAB   Flat piece of leather worn on the string hand to protect the fingers and provide a smooth release.

FISTMELE   A term describing the height of the fist with the thumb extended, used in measuring the distance between the bow and the string when the bow is braced, usually a distance of 6 to 7".

FLETCHINGS   The feathers on an arrow.

FLIGHT SHOOTING   The effort to shoot an arrow the farthest distance possible.

FLU-FLU   An arrow with an oversize fletching used in hunting or archery games.

FOLLOW THE STRING   The tendency of a bow to follow the curves of the bow when it is unstrung; to become curved toward the belly when not in use; to become set.

GAP   A method of aiming by estimating the distance between a selected point and the target.

GROUND QUIVER   A receptacle on the ground or floor that holds the arrows the archer is not shooting; often combined with a bow rack.

GROUPING   The close clustering of arrows on the target.

HANDLE   Ther center part of the bow held by the archer.

HANGING ARROW   An arrow which does not penetrate the face of the target sufficiently to hold it in; an arrow which hangs from the target face.

HEN FEATHERS   The two feathers on an arrow not at right angles to the nock.

HIT   Strike on the target in the scoring area.

HOLD   Steadily keeping an arrow at full draw before the release.

KEEPER   A piece of string, leather, plastic, or other material that holds the string to the nock when the bow is unstrung.

LADY PARAMOUNT   The woman who presides over the women's shooting line.

LIMB   Either part of the bow, from handle to tip, upper or lower nock.

LOOSE   To release the fully drawn bow string.

MAIL MATCH   Competition shot in different places, the results of which are forwarded to the tournament director.

NOCK   The grooves at the end of the limbs of the bow into which the string is fitted; also the groove at the end of the arrow that fits onto the string; the act of placing the arrow on the string.

NOCKING POINT   The point on the string at which the nock of the arrow is placed.

OVERDRAW   Drawing the arrow until the pile is within the belly of the bow; drawing the bow beyond the required length of an arrow; drawing the bow string farther than the length indicated by the manufacturer for that particular bow.

PERFECT END   All arrows shot into the center of the target in one end.

PETTICOAT   The edge of the target beyond the outside ring; counts as a miss.

PILE   The tip of the arrow; the metal point of the arrow.

PINCH   To squeeze the nock of the arrow.

PINSIGHT   A device on the bow used for sighting and aiming.

PLUCKING   Jerking the right hand away from the string on the release.

POINT BLANK RANGE   The distance at which the point of aim and the center of the target coincide. The distance at which one can aim directly at the center of the target and hit the center of the target.

POINT OF AIM   The point at which one should aim to hit the target; a mark, used when sighting, upon which the tip of the arrow rests.

QUIVER   A device for holding arrows.

RANGE   The distance to be shot; the shooting area; an archery ground, indoors or out.

RANGE FINDER   A device for finding an already established point of aim.

REBOUND   An arrow that bounces off the scoring area of the target. It is assigned a value of seven or five.

RELEASE   To allow the fingers to roll off the fully drawn string, sending the arrow on its way.

ROUND   The name used to indicate shooting a specific number of arrows at a designated distance or distances.

SELF BOW   A bow made of one kind of material.

SERVING   The wrapping of string around the bow string in the areas which receive the most wear: the nocking point and the loops.

SHAFT   The main part of the arrow.

SHOOTING LINE   The common line straddled by all archers when shooting.

SPINE   Refers to an arrow's strength and resiliency.

STRINGING   Bracing a bow; securing the string correctly in the nocks.

TAB   A protection for the fingers used on the string.

TACKLE   An all-inclusive term for archery equipment.

TARGET CAPTAIN   The archer at each target who is in charge.

TARGET FACE   The front cover of a target, painted with the regulation rings or designs.

TASSEL   A piece of fiber or wool yarn used to clean arrows.

TELEGRAPHIC MATCH   See "mail match."

TOXOPHILITE   Lover of archery; one skilled in archery.

TOXOPHILUS   The first book on archery, written by Roger Ascham in 1544.

TRAJECTORY   The path an arrow describes in flight.

VANE   A feather on the arrow.

WEIGHT   The total pull, measured in pounds, required to draw a bow the length of its arrow; of an arrow, actual weight in grains.

Tools
of the
Trade

Good equipment, like a good friend, adds to the pleasure of life. Both are a source of enjoyment and both are chosen for their qualities. The choice of a friend is a very personal thing and involves a number of intangibles. Selection of appropriate archery gear is not so complex, but it does require knowledge of the paraphernalia if intelligent decisions are to be made. Equipment is usually provided by the school or athletics department when archery is a regular program offering. Physical characteristics, such as strength and length of arms, should be considered in an attempt to match the available equipment to each individual archer.

Active participation in any sport requires certain basic implements. Archery equipment, called *tackle*, includes bows, arrows, and a number of accessories. Each piece of apparatus is available in several sizes, shapes, and materials as well as in a wide range of prices. Variety may be the spice of life, but it can also serve to confuse. The shooter needs to have some realistic criteria in mind when selecting suitable tackle.

ESSENTIALS

Arrows

The novice probably thinks of the bow as the most important piece of essential equipment. Obviously, it is impossible to enjoy the sport of archery without an implement to cast the projectile. While the value of a good bow should not be underestimated, many expert shooters give priority to arrow selection. Great care should be taken to select sets that are matched in length, weight, and spine. Inexpensive, poor quality arrows are not conducive to good scores, no matter how excellent the bow from which they are launched. Matched arrows will fly consistently to the mark, unless the archer causes them to do otherwise. Unmatched arrows tend to vary in flight pattern. At short ranges, the use of unmatched arrows may not hamper the beginner, but as the distance from the target increases, the effect of mismatching becomes more evident. Although arrows employed for hunting, flight shooting, target, and other forms of archery are similar in basic structure, certain aspects of design vary.

Arrow Length. Intended use, body structure, and shooting style determine the arrow length suitable for each individual. Ideally, if the arrow is of correct length, the tip will be even with the back of the bow when at full draw. In selecting hunting arrows, the length must allow for extension of the specially designed point beyond the bow. Individual draw length is arrived at in several ways.

Yardstick. A yardstick is placed on the center of the breast bone (sternum) and both arms, palms inward, are extended forward without stretching. Arrow length is read at the place the finger tips touch the yardstick. A variation of this technique uses a 30" arrow marked for every

Figure 4.1   Parts of an arrow.

inch from the pile end. This method is serviceable but only approximates the desired length.

Arm Span. The arms are extended sideways and a tape measure is used to determine the span across the body between the tips of the middle fingers. Arrow length is estimated by calculating 38 per cent of the figure obtained or read from a conversion chart if one is available.

Draw Measure. The bow is drawn to the preferred anchor. Distance from the string to the back of the bow is measured with a yardstick or tape measure.

Bow Device. The most accurate means of ascertaining correct arrow length is the bow device. This specially constructed piece of apparatus consists of a calibrated arrow shaft attached to the string of a lightweight bow. The arrow moves back through the guide attached to the bow as the string is brought to the intended anchor. Arrow length is read off at the mark closest to the back of the bow. This method allows for variations in the anchor and body position preferred by the archer and is used by most professional archery shops.

An inexperienced shooter is wise to select arrows that are a little too long (about an inch) until he has established his shooting style. The extra length provides a safety margin in case an overdraw is made (a common occurrence with beginners) and allows for adjustments when experimenting with anchor and stance positions. Matched sets of arrows are all exactly the same in length.

Arrow Weight. Matched arrows weigh within five grains of one another. Superior grade wooden arrows are available in matched weights, but this cannot be determined by visual examination. Even though wooden shafts are of equal thickness, the density of the material may produce a weight variation. Quality control in the manufacturing of aluminum and fiberglass shafts provides for more accurate matching in arrow weights. While a slight weight variance is not of singular concern in the initial stages of learning, it assumes more importance as the archer develops his ability to send his arrows off in a consistent manner. An arrow's errant flight is not easily detected by sight. Advanced archers often identify arrows with special marks or number decals and systematically record where each shot lands. Inconsistent hits may be due to weight variance or other factors such as improper spine, lack of shaft straightness, or feather damage. Deviation in weight is associated with high and low arrow flight.

Shaft. A good shaft is straight and has a smooth finish without rough spots or edges. Piles, nocks, and feathers are firmly attached, and the entire arrow is free from glue deposits. An attractive crest facilitates identification and provides aesthetic appeal.

Wooden shafted arrows are usually less expensive than those made of other materials and are often purchased in quantity by schools. Norwegian pine is the preferred wood, but Port Oxford cedar, although somewhat less durable, is commonly used. Birch shafts are least expensive but the tendency to warp easily makes purchase a poor long-term investment.

Fiberglass shafts have become extremely popular recently. Characteristics such as lightness, durability, and resistance to warping hastened the adoption of this shaft material by many institutions and individuals. Matched sets of fiberglass arrows are considered to perform better than matched sets of wooden arrows.

The most expensive arrows are made with aluminum shafts and are usually selected by the more serious tournament archer. Aluminum alloys, developed through exhaustive research by manufacturers, allow arrows to be produced with extremely fine tolerances. Metal shafts are not subject to warp but have a tendency to bend if stepped on or upon impact with hard objects. Although original straightness can be restored with the use of specially designed tools or, in some cases, by hand, the bending factor is a consideration in selection.

Spine. Flexibility or stiffness of the arrow's shaft is called *spine.* Arrows matched for spine are within 0.02° of each other in deflection when subjected to measurement on a spinetester. Erratic grouping results unless spine is compatible with the poundage of the bow and the type and weight of the arrow. Proper spine specifications have been regulated by manufacturers.

The archer who has developed uniformity in his technique but fails to have his arrows cluster in a consistent manner, should suspect improper arrow spine as a possible cause. Arrows that are too stiff brush the bow on release resulting in some loss of impetus and deviation in direction. Shafts that are too flexible produce right-left errors as the arrow fails to stabilize in flight.

Fletching. The feathers or vanes at the end of the shaft stabilize the flying arrow. Each vane is of the same size, shape, and stiffness on a quality arrow. It is possible for the number of feathers used in the fletch to vary but the most common arrangement is three. Two feathers of similar color called *hen feathers*, with an odd colored *cock feather* at right angles to the groove in the arrow's nock, are spaced symmetrically on the shaft. Identical characteristics of curve or straightness are considered in selecting feathers for matched sets of arrows.

The size and shape of the fletching may be altered for special circumstances. A flu-flu fletch is often used for hunting small game because the exaggerated size of the feathers slows the arrow quickly, allowing easy retrieval if the intended target is missed. Plastic vanes are available, although their use is not widespread at the present time.

Piles. The tip or point of the arrow is called the *pile*. The primary consideration in selecting a particular type of pile for an arrow is the intended use of the projectile. Whatever type is selected, care has to be taken to see that it is securely attached to the shaft and correctly aligned. Target piles are bullet-shaped

Figure 4.2 Types of fletchings.

A. *Target*
B. *Hunting*
C. *Flu-Flu*

or parallel, the latter being preferable. The field point type of pile is constructed to suit the conditions encountered in this form of shooting. Hunting tips are found in many shapes and sizes, and vary according to the kind of game the archer expects to hit.

Bows

Bows are constructed of many materials and come in different sizes, shapes, weights, and lengths. Although some bows are multipurpose, selection of a bow is usually made with a primary purpose in mind. Hunting bows are heavier, and often shorter, than target or field archery bows. The competitive target archer, who may send more than two hundred arrows flying towards a stationary target in a day's shooting, would seldom select the same bow as the hunter stalking large game.

Bow design has been greatly influenced by the development of fiberglass, plastics, resins, and strong epoxy adhesives. The traditional wooden long bow, first used at the Battle of Hastings, has been replaced by the more efficient composite recurve type. Wood provides the elasticity essential for good *cast*, but it has a tendency to lose its shape over long periods. Solid fiberglass is strong and durable but without the characteristic smoothness of fine wooden bows. Composite bows incorporate the best features of both fiberglass and wood and are considered to be the best available at the present time. Shape, length, weight-in-hand, draw weight, and materials used in construction are factors to consider when purchasing or selecting a bow for personal use.

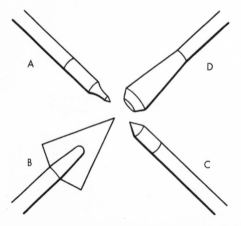

Figure 4.3   Types of piles or points.

A. *Field Point*
B. *Hunting Head*
C. *Target Point*
D. *Blunt for small animals or archery games.*

Long or Straight-Limbed Bows. The long or straight-limbed bow is still commonly used in many schools and camps. It is usually constructed of a single stave of material with a handle of some kind separating the limbs. Some bows are reinforced with a backing to add strength and aid in retention of shape. Most long bows are designed so that they can be used by left-handed as well as right-handed shooters. If an arrow shelf is not provided, the archer is required to use the upper part of the bow hand as support for the arrow. Unless the handle or grip is specially constructed, the archer is almost forced to use a low wrist or palm hold on the bow. Although some archers prefer the straight-limbed bow, it is considered more difficult to master than the recurve type. Generally speaking, the long bow seems to have many disadvantages; its design does not make it the most efficient or the most durable. The lack of a sight window, which allows for better aiming and a more centered shot, coupled with the uneven stress built up within the limbs during the draw, adds to its negative features.

Recurve Bows. The distinct advantages of the recurve type bow have led to its almost universal adoption by today's archery enthusiasts. All recurves are not the same, however, and some should really not enjoy the distinction of being classified as such. To be considered a true recurve, the string must actually touch the *belly* of the bow for 2 or 3" in the area adjacent to the *nocks*. If a bow does not have this characteristic, it operates in essentially the same manner as the long bow. If the bow is properly designed, the curves at the extreme ends "open" with the draw, thus providing additional leverage and increasing the potential velocity of the projectile.

Figure 4.4 Parts of the bow.

The recurve bow is considered to be a "fast bow" because a well executed recurve sends the arrow off at greater speed than a long bow of the same draw weight. A quality recurve bow also tends to be a "smooth bow," that is, it does not become noticeably harder to pull or "stack-up" as the archer draws through the last few inches to his anchor point. In addition, the form of the handle or riser fits more comfortably in the bow hand. This configuration is conducive to the use of a high or extended wrist when gripping the bow and also aids in achieving a more relaxed bow arm. The cutaway section, called a *sight window*, allows for the inclusion of an arrow shelf or rest, and produces a more centered shot.

Recurves are constructed from a single piece of wood formed by application of heat and pressure. Solid fiberglass recurve bows are popular for school use since they are relatively inexpensive and extremely durable. Composite or laminated bows, made of layers of wood and fiberglass, combine the most desirable features of both materials to produce a strong, durable implement which has good elasticity, retains its shape well, and gives consistent performance.

Continued use of exactly the same bow for each day's shooting is advantageous. Each bow has its own unique shooting characteristics. Two bows may be exactly alike in design, length, and draw weight and still cast the arrows differently. Use of the same equipment allows the individual to become throughly acquainted with his tackle.

Bow Length and Weight. Bows are manufactured in lengths from 52 to 72"; lengths of 64 to 70" are favored for target type archery. A longer bow adds weight that is helpful in steadying the bow hand and aiding in smoothing the release. The added "weight-in-hand" (the actual avoirdupois weight of the bow), however, may produce fatigue if actual shooting is carried on over long periods. The force required to pull a bow to a full draw for a given arrow length is called *draw weight*.

Weight-in-hand is important to target shooters since holding a heavy bow may hasten arm fatigue. Draw weight is important to all archers. Unless otherwise specified, most bow weights are given as the number of pounds necessary to pull a

28" arrow to a full draw. If a shorter arrow is shot, the effort required is correspondingly lessened. Construction characteristics of the bow determine the exact amount of poundage necessary to draw arrows of different lengths. With some recurves the differential is as much as 2 pounds per inch of draw. This means that a shooter using a 25" arrow with a bow weighed in at 25 pounds exerts force equivalent to 19 pounds when at full draw. Conversely, an archer drawing a 30" arrow with the same bow requires pressure equal to 29 pounds.

It is logical to assume that scoring effectiveness is enhanced with use of a heavier bow. The added velocity allows a flatter trajectory. This factor becomes increasingly important as the distance from the target becomes greater. However, while logic might dictate that doubling the bow weight increases the arrow velocity accordingly, research shows that a 100 per cent increase in bow weight produces, at best, a 25 per cent increase in arrow speed.

Individual muscle strength is of primary importance in bow weight determination. In their zeal to score well, many archers (particularly beginners) have a tendency to "over bow" themselves. The novice is wise to select a fairly light bow, one that he can draw easily and shoot comfortably. Development of proper form is often sacrificed to bad habits when compensating for lack of sufficient muscular strength. Hunching of the forward shoulder or locking of the bow arm are symptomatic of a bow that is too strong for the archer. Since the upper back muscles, which do most of the work during the draw, are not usually developed to the extent needed at the onset of shooting, it is important to start with a light bow. Increases in bow weight are made gradually, about 1 to 3 pounds at a time, and only as muscular strength develops through use.

Arm Guards

The arm guard could be considered an accessory, since it is not absolutely essential to the shooting act. However, the protection it provides for the bow arm is essential if good form is to be developed. The arm guard is worn below the elbow, near the wrist of the bow arm. Prudent use of this plastic or leather shield prevents painful bruises that result if the string strikes the area. The added protection builds confidence and promotes consistent form. Failure to cover the arm properly could lead to flinching or other detrimental habits.

Finger Tabs or Gloves

The fingers of the string hand are covered with finger tabs or specially designed shooting gloves. Friction between the fingers and the bow string can produce sores or blisters when shooting for prolonged periods. Tabs or gloves protect the areas subject to hurt and aid in developing a smooth, consistent release. Many novice archers experience difficulty in adjusting to the use of finger tabs or gloves and tend to disregard their importance. Careful attention to proper fit and a little patience is all that is necessary to overcome any initial discomfort.

ACCESSORIES

Quivers

Metal ground quivers which hold the arrows upright and provide a rest for the bow when not in use are desirable pieces of tackle. Most schools provide a ground quiver and some

Figure 4.5 Glove, finger tab, and arm guard.

institutions also issue a hip or belt receptacle for holding arrows. Other types of quivers fit across the back, on the leg, or attach to the bow itself.

Sights

Mechanical devices secured to the bow aid the archer in aiming his shots. The variety of sights available is almost limitless. Each sight is constructed so that adjustments can be made for bow elevation and *windage* (right-left). Simple post sights are made from inexpensive materials such as cork, self-adhesive weather stripping, tongue depressors, and large bead head dressmaker straight pins. A strip of material is attached to the back or belly of the bow and a pin is inserted on the arrow side to serve as the post. The pin is moved up or down and in or out, as needed to correct distance and directional errors.

Other Accessories

Additional accessories serve a number of different functions. A bow case protects the bow during storage and can be purchased or easily made from a piece of flannel material.

Figure 4.6   Quivers.

Figure 4.7   Sights.

Tackle boxes are convenient for storage and transporting arrows and other shooting equipment. Chest guards, cleaning tassels, string keepers, bow tip protectors, bow strings, powder dispensers, anchor locks, "kissing" buttons, and mechanical devices that indicate when exact draw length is reached are some of the many supplemental pieces of gear. As interest in active participation grows, so usually does the list of tackle the archer feels is necessary for maximum enjoyment.

CARE OF EQUIPMENT

It is relatively expensive for a school to provide good basic archery tackle. A conscientious instructor should attempt to secure the best possible equipment with the money available. He knows that good tackle facilitates learning and adds to the enjoyment of the participant. Whether the archer has his own equipment or is using tackle provided by an institution, attention to proper care and repair will significantly increase its useful life and provide a margin of safety. Several pertinent points are listed below.

Bows

1. Brace the bows correctly. (Proper procedure is described in the following chapter.)
2. Unstring the bows when not in use. Some bows will take a set if stored in a braced position; others are not affected.
3. Bows should be suspended vertically, or placed horizontally across pegs, in a cool area that has some degree of humidity.
4. Storage in a case protects the bow from scratches and prevents excess moisture from accumulating.
5. Periodic applications of quality furniture or floor wax will protect the bow's finish. Use of beeswax on the string and paraffin on the servings will minimize fraying. Frayed strings should always be replaced.

6. Bows should not be overdrawn or the string released without an arrow.
7. Bows should not be dropped or laid on the ground to prevent damage by being stepped on or affected by residual moisture.
8. Bows should be "warmed up" before actual use by drawing several times and letting down easily.
9. Bows should be checked for proper fistmele at periodic intervals.

Arrows

1. Arrows should be retrieved and carried by the shaft and not by the feathers.
2. Arrows should be stored in racks or in specially designed cases.
3. Arrows should be checked for damage and wiped clean after each end. Cracked or splintered arrows should be destroyed immediately to prevent possible injury by use.
4. Replacement of loose or damaged piles, nocks, and fletchings is essential for safety as well as accuracy.
5. Application of wax to the shaft prolongs the life of the finish.

SUGGESTED TASKS FOR THE STUDENT

1. Check your archery vocabulary by naming and identifying the various parts of the bow and arrow.
2. Measure yourself for arrow length using at least two of the methods described. Record the length indicated by each method.
3. Draw bows of several different weights and note the weight most comfortable for you at this time. Repeat the procedure after several weeks of shooting.
4. Calculate or estimate the force you exert when drawing a bow of a given weight for your arrow length.
5. Determine whether or not your set of arrows is matched. Record or list the points of similarity and/or

variation. (NOTE: Most schools do not own spine-testers or arrow scales. The instructor can usually provide information about the spine and weight of arrows. The more curious or creative student may seek ways of applying knowledge from scientific disciplines to the solution of the problem.)

6. Shoot bows of different weights and design. Note the differences in arrow speed and trajectory for shots at given distances.

7. Shoot arrows of different spine and weight from the same bow. Attempt to determine which arrows are most compatible with that bow.

8. Find out how the fistmele is measured for your particular bow, and check the bow for correct string distance. Make any necessary adjustments in string length.

9. Check your understanding of archery terminology used in the text by writing out definitions and comparing these with the glossary provided earlier in this book.

10. List the features you would look for if you were considering the purchase of equipment for your own personal use.

11. Describe how you would care for your own personal equipment.

12. Replace the nock, feathers and/or pile of an arrow.

The Fundamentals

Some archers have developed distinct and unique ways of shooting. It is often possible to identify an individual merely by watching his performance. Factors that influence shooting style include personal preference, physical characteristics, equipment design, and advocacy of a particular theory of shooting. Whatever the reason, the ability to produce a successful performance is based upon familiarity with the tackle and a thorough understanding of the principles governing its use.

Power, necessary to hurl any missile, must be provided in some manner. The bow is given the needed potential energy by pulling on the string causing the limbs to assume an unnatural position. As the string is released, the limbs move forward supplying force to the arrow. Concisely stated, shooting an arrow involves pulling the bow string and letting it go! The entire process is simplicity itself, or so it seems. Closer scrutiny reveals a more complex operation. Certain prerequisite acts are performed before the arrow is placed on the string. Other movements precede the draw and follow the release. The basic process is repeated precisely and consistently to obtain desired results.

PREPARING THE BOW

The bow and string should be checked before each day's shooting. Faulty strings should be replaced, and bows in need of repair should not be used. The bow must be *braced*, or strung, before it is ready for use. Bracing increases tension in the limbs by forcing them to assume a greater bend than normal. Stringing is accomplished by a proper application of force to produce the necessary leverage. Some schools have mechanical bracing devices that produce mechanical advantage and allow bows to be strung with a minimum of physical effort. Such devices prolong the useful life of the equipment and are recommended. Manual bracing is accomplished by either the push-pull or step-through methods.

Figure 5.1 Push-pull bracing.

Push-Pull Method

Most manufacturers recommend the push-pull method for both straight limbed and recurve bows. The lower limb is immobilized by placing it against the instep (inside) of the foot. One hand pulls the center of the bow outward while the other hand simultaneously forces the upper limb downward. Once sufficient bend has been obtained, the fingers work the loop of the string into the upper nock. Figure 5.1 illustrates the position and means of applying pressure.

Summary of the Push-Pull Method

1. Check to see that the string is correctly seated in the nock of the lower limb.
2. Assume a comfortable stance with the feet apart.
3. Place the lower end of the bow, back up, against the instep of the foot. Take care to see that the tip is not resting on the ground.
4. Grasp the handle of the bow with the hand on the same side as the foot used to steady the lower limb.
5. Place the palm area of the free hand on the upper limb so that the fingers are in contact with the loop of the string. The thumb and index fingers should be free to manipulate the string.
6. Apply a pulling force with the lower hand as the upper hand presses down on the upper limb.
7. Work the loop of the string into the upper nock with the fingers once the bow has sufficient bend.
8. Check to see that both of the loops are properly secured in the nocks and the string aligned with the bow. Be sure to hold the bow well away from the face and body.

Step-Through Method

The step-through method is used with heavier bows or when the archer lacks sufficient strength to use other means. The lower limb is stabilized by placing the back of the bow across the ankle area. The other leg is lifted through the space between the string and the belly of the bow. The bow moves to a position behind the body so that the handle or riser rests high on the rear of the upper thigh. The bow is bent by applying force in a forward direction and the string slipped into the nock with the free hand.

Summary of Step-Through Bracing

1. Check the lower nock for proper string seating.
2. Assume a comfortable upright stance.
3. Place the back of the lower limb across the ankle of one foot so that the belly of the bow is away from the body.
4. Step the other leg through the area between the belly of the bow and the string.
5. Move the bow to a position behind the stepping leg so that the handle or riser rests high behind the thigh.
6. Raise the heel of the supporting foot slightly to aid in preventing torque or twisting of the bow limbs.
7. Bend the upper limb forward with one hand and move the loop of the string into the nock with the other hand.
8. Check both nocks for proper string insertion and alignment.

Figure 5.2   Step-through method.

Safety

Once the bow limbs are bent they possess potential energy. If the string has not been placed in the nocks correctly, the force could be released unexpectedly. Examine the strings seeing that the loops are placed in the right way. The bow should be held well away from the face in such a way that the limbs will not contact any part of the face or body if they should suddenly slip free. Remember, bow tips are rather pointed, so a little care will avoid a serious or painful injury!

THE SHOOTING ACT

Shooting should be thought of and practiced as an integrated whole. However, an understanding of the interrelatedness of each of the subsequent parts helps in analyzing performance. Each part affects the end result in some significant manner. At times it is necessary to practice a particular aspect of the total act in correcting performance; whenever this happens some relearning takes place as the parts are again put together.

The archer should strive to arrive at a definite pattern in reaching for the arrow, placing it on the string, raising the bow arm, drawing, aiming, holding, and releasing the string. If the rhythm is broken at any time, it is better to "let down" and start over than to try to adjust along the way.

The procedure closely resembles the ritual used by many golfers as they prepare to hit the ball: the distance to the green is estimated; the club selected; the feet aligned; the grip checked; the body and foot positions again observed; the waggle performed; and then the ball hit. The whole process is repeated in the same sequence and time structure every time a shot is made. Observe professional golfers on television sometime; you can practically count out the beat. This systematic approach helps to establish the feeling that everything is right. A definite established procedure provides feedback and allows detection of possible errors before they become misses at the target.

Stance

The initial body and foot position, called the *stance*, is important because it produces the most effective posture for applying a "sideways" force. The body assumes a balanced position that helps to steady the bow arm during the draw and release. Either a square or open stance can be used. In the more traditional square stance, the feet straddle the shooting line so that an imaginary line extended across the toes points to the center of the target. The open stance is accomplished by drawing the forward foot back about 6" from the square position. If the open stance is used, the hips and shoulders must also turn so that they are in line with the toes. In target archery the hips and shoulders may point to the target next to the one used for shooting when the feet are in the open position. Either stance requires an evenly balanced, upright posture with the head turned so that it is facing the intended hitting area. The open stance moves the bow arm away from the string a bit and is helpful in building a beginning archer's confidence. Once the stance position is determined it should remain the same each and every time an arrow is nocked, drawn, and released. After

Figure 5.3 Stance.

some shooting experience, experimentation with different foot positions and weight distributions aids in establishing the most effective individual positions. In some cases, the instructor may recommend changes based on certain physical characteristics or to help compensate for subtle errors in other parts of the form.

Grip

Design characteristics of the handle effect the grip used to hold the bow. A pistol handle or riser readily lends itself to the use of a loose fingered, high wrist position. A standard handle serves to promote the use of a low wrist or "palming" grip. The extended wrist position can be mastered with most bows and is the one recommended.

To achieve the high or extended wrist position, "shake hands" with the bow so that it rests in the "V" formed by the thumb and index finger. The fingers are relatively loose and the bow is not actually gripped but braced in the groove so that the wrist is slightly above or directly behind the hand. The arm is fully extended with the forward shoulder and elbow down and rotated back slightly. If the bow arm is in the correct position, flexion of the elbow will cause the lower arm to move directly in toward the body like a door swinging inward. If the arm is incorrectly positioned, the bow will move diagonally upward or downward depending on the shoulder and elbow position. To avoid dropping the bow at release the fingers of the bow hand are pointed slightly downward and light pressure is applied to the sides of the bow by the thumb and index finger. Some people have the tips of the thumb and index finger touching as they encircle the bow.

The low wrist position has the bow braced against the fleshy part of the palm with the wrist slightly below the upper part of the hand. Many people use this grip successfully, but it does make it a little more difficult to put the elbow and shoulder in the best position. The beginning archer is urged to master the high or extended wrist technique because of the advantages afforded by better arm and shoulder positioning. In addition, the low wrist position tends to produce more and quicker fatigue of the arm muscles.

Failure to achieve a good grip and proper bow arm alignment will result in serious shooting errors. The slightest movement of the arm will cause the arrow to miss the intended impact area by several inches or even feet, depending on the distance from the target. Painful slaps or bruises result when the string hits the bow arm and this can seriously effect the archer's confidence. Care should be exercised to see that the wrist is correctly aligned behind the hand (not rotated inward or outward) and that the elbow is not locked or stiff.

Nocking

There are a number of ways to place the arrow on the string. Some people grasp the end of the nock, others hold the arrow by its shaft. The bow is held in a low or horizontal position so the back of the bow hand is visible (palm down). Two things should be kept in mind when nocking the arrow. First, place the arrow in exactly the same place on the string each time. Second, place the cock feather so that it is away from the bow. At first the arrow is nocked at a 90° angle with the string. But as shooting experience progresses, a nocking

Figure 5.4 Grip: high and low wrist.

point 1/8" to 1/4" above the perpendicular is used. A nocking point on the string helps to ensure replication of arrow placement. A piece of masking tape can be substituted if the nocking point has not been served (wound). There are a number of commercially manufactured nocking points available which are easily fixed on the string. The arrow is usually nocked below, not on, the nocking indicator.

Grasping the String

Once the nock of the arrow is seated on the serving, the three string fingers reach under the string so that the index finger rests above the arrow with the two other fingers below. Either the "shallow" or "deep" hook positions are used. The term *hook* refers to the position of the fingers, not the position of the hand itself. The shallow hook is the one most commonly taught. The string is placed in such a position that it rests just

Figure 5.5   Nocking positions and grasping the string.

above or in the groove of the first joint, not on the very tips of the fingers. The knuckles are not bent; the back of the hand is flat and in line with the lower arm; the thumb and little fingers are in toward the palm.

The deep hook differs from the shallow in that the string is allowed to rest between the first and second finger joints. The deep hook is often easier for beginners to use and is not really disadvantageous in perfecting a smooth release. Experimentation with the deep hook will demonstrate that a smooth release is possible once the archer learns to simply relax his fingers.

Both grasps require that the thumb and little finger be moved toward the palm so that they are out of the way. Touching the tip of the little finger and thumb together may prove helpful. The hand position resembles that used in the Boy Scout salute. Whichever string finger position produces the best release is the one to use. The arrow is not squeezed or gripped between the fingers but rather caressed.

Drawing

The draw may be initiated in a number of ways. The bow can be raised above the head, arm fully or partially extended, and the string drawn back as the bow is lowered to shooting position. Beginners should learn to assume the proper bow arm position before developing an individual draw style. The bow is raised from the side of the body to a vertical position with the extended arm about shoulder height. The elbow and shoulder are rotated down and back. *Canting* or tilting the bow slightly at first helps to keep the arrow in proper position. Beginners usually have trouble keeping the arrow on the bow; the tendency to squeeze the nock causes the arrow to move sideways away from the bow. As the draw is started, this pressure becomes greater and can prove to be a real problem. The arrow must rest lightly between the fingers; in fact, it is a good idea to move the upper finger away slightly from the arrow. The index finger of the bow hand can be used to steady the arrow during the draw but is removed when the anchor position is reached.

The forward shoulder position is often overlooked. A poor shoulder position is not always evident until the string is actually started back. Hunching of the bow shoulder is indicative of equipment that is too strong for the archer. In such cases a lighter bow should be used until sufficient strength is attained to handle the equipment. Once the bow arm is in proper position, the string is drawn back by the upper arm, back, and upper shoulder muscles. The fingers of the hand merely act as hooks and do not supply force for the draw. The string is moved back in a smooth and deliberate manner. Taking a deep breath, in coordination with the pull itself, during the drawing phase seems to assist some people. Think of moving the scapula or wings of the back together as if to pinch or hold something between the shoulder blades.

The idea of a perfectly straight line extending from the tip of the arrow, down its shaft, along the back of the hand and lower arm to the elbow, seems to be firmly established in the literature on shooting technique. Observation shows that this straight line does not usually exist. If the proper muscles are used, the tip of the drawing elbow will be slightly above the arrow.

Anchor

It is extremely important that the arrow be drawn exactly the same distance each time. The drawn bow can be likened to the powder charge in a bullet: if the powder charge in two bullets is different, they will not fly in exactly the same manner. To have a consistent propelling force for the arrow, the arm position and the anchor point must be the same for each arrow shot. Once this is accomplished, aiming becomes the variable in which adjustments are made for distance and direction. If the arrow is not drawn back to the same point each time, the potential velocity is increased or decreased depending upon the variation in draw length. Errors of this nature become more evident as the distance from the target increases.

Anchor positions are generally classified as high and low. One high anchor has the tip of the index finger drawn to the corner of the sighting eye. This gives the feeling of sighting almost directly along the shaft of the arrow to the target and is considered, by some, to aid in aiming. Hunters, field archers and instinctive shooters usually employ a high anchor technique. The most common high anchor has the tip of the index finger at the corner of the mouth so that the top of the hand rests along the lower part of the cheek bone. Placement of the forefinger in the corner of the mouth helps to establish a definite point of contact and aids in lining up the arrow under the sighting eye.

In low anchor the forefinger rests directly under the jawbone so that the string is in line with the center of the face. The string actually touches the tip of the nose and the center of the chin. Many archers purse their lips and actually kiss the string. If the contour of the fact is such that it is difficult to get the finger under the chin, it may be placed along the side of the jawbone so that its tip rests in the center of the chin. The low anchor position has advantages in sighing and allows for greater cast. The low anchor is favored by target archers and most expert freestyle shooters. Either anchor can be successfully used in any situation.

The high anchor is usually taught first. As the student gains in experience and becomes more familiar with the use and functions of the equipment, the low anchor is introduced. A common fallacy among novice archers is that a different anchor point or draw length is needed for each shooting distance. If the arrow is to fly at the same velocity each time, the draw length and anchor must be the same each time. Adjustments for distance and directional errors are made in the aim, not by variations in the holding position. Why use "by guess and by gosh" when it is possible to determine how much and how far! Why attempt to learn what amounts to five or six different skills, when it is necessary to learn only one? Once the shooter is familiar with the relationships of trajectory, draw length, anchor point, and aim, the logic of a consistent position becomes evident.

Aiming

The use of some type of device, such as a bow sight or a point-of-aim marker characterizes freestyle (sight) shooting. Absence of an aiming device is identified with instinctive or bare bow shooting. Aiming enables an archer to be more accurate in his arrow placement. Different procedures are used by different archers with varying degrees of success. The advantages provided by a bow sight cannot be overstated. However, any mechanical instrument or device is of little help until the archer becomes proficient in the performance of the fundamentals and is able to group his arrows. For this reason beginning archers are usually introduced to shooting and aiming by the instinctive or bare bow method.

Bare Bow or Instinctive Aiming.   To shoot without a sight or point-of-aim marker, the bow is drawn to the anchor (usually a high one at first) and the eyes are focused on the exact center of the intended target. The elevation of the bow arm almost automatically adjusts itself as the archer concentrates on the intended impact area rather than on the tip of the arrow or the hand. After the first couple of arrows are released, feedback

Figure 5.6   High and low anchor positions. Note: Archer is using arrow with four vanes.

provides information to indicate how the bow arm must be moved (up, down, and/or to either side). Accurate visual shooting depends upon consistent form, good eyesight, well-developed depth perception, and kinesthetic awareness on the part of the shooter.

Point of Aim. Point of aim is probably the most commonly taught means of aiming the bow. Unfortunately this method has limitations and other procedures are more appropriate. Point of aim should only serve as a temporary aiming procedure. The tip of an arrow is used like a post in a sight and aimed at some spot in front of, on, or above the target. At anchor, the tip of the arrow is usually well below the sighting eye. The aiming spot selected for a given distance depends upon the height of the shooter, length of the arrow drawn, and bow weight. It is not exactly the same for each individual. There is only one distance from the target when the tip of the arrow can be aimed directly at its center. This distance is called *point blank range* and may not coincide with any of the established shooting lines. At relatively short distances, the sighting spot is on the ground in front of the target. As the range is increased, the spot moves closer to the target. At extremely long distances, or with very light bows, an aiming point above the impact area may be needed. Point of aim for each distance is determined by shooting several arrows and examining the groupings which occur. Clusters below the

Figure 5.7   Point of aim. Note: Arrow trajectory would be different if high anchor were used necessitating different points of aim for the same distances.

center of the target indicate the need to move the aiming point farther away from the archer. High groupings or arrows over the target necessitate moving the spot closer to the archer. Once the aiming spots are located for different distances, a range finder is constructed. This device eliminates the need to experiment each day of shooting.

CONSTRUCTION AND USE OF A RANGE FINDER

Construction of a Range Finder

1. Use a stick about 1" wide and 5 or 6" long. (A tongue depressor is commonly used.)
2. Stand on the shooting line at the same spot from which the point of aim for that distance was determined.
3. Mark an "X" on the bottom of the stick and a line across the top.
4. Hold an arrow out from the chin at the same height as the arrow which would be aimed.
5. Place the "X" on the stick on the tip of the arrow and sight along the stick until the line at the top is in the center of the gold.
6. Look down the stick to find the spot where the point of aim is visible along the side.
7. Mark the spot where the point of aim occurs on the stick with a line and the particular distance.

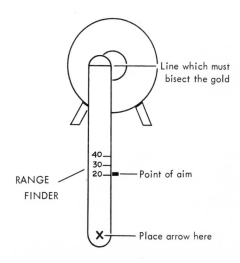

Figure 5.8   Range finder.

Use of a Range Finder

In using a range finder, the following procedure should be observed:

1. Stand on the shooting line, holding the arrow on the spot on the chin.
2. Place the top line on the stick in the center of the gold.
3. Look down the stick until the line for that particular distance is found. Note the spot on the ground where the point of aim should be placed.
4. Place the point of aim on the ground at the determined spot.

Gap Methods of Aiming. Pre-gap and post-gap aim are similar to point of aim in that the archer uses the tip of the arrow to sight to a selected spot. The distance between the desired point of entry and the aiming spot is called the gap. In pre-gap aiming, the bow is raised to shooting position and the tip of the arrow aligned with a predetermined spot before the draw. Once the bow arm position is established, the eyes shift to the intended target and intently focus there. The draw and subsequent release is made without altering body or head position. Post-gap aim differs from pre-gap only in that the

Figure 5.9 Gap aiming. Note: Broken lines represent gap after draw. Solid lines represent gap before the draw.

arrow tip is placed on a spot at full draw. Both gap systems differ from point of aim in that once the arrow is lined up, the eyes focus on the intended target, not on the aiming spot. Adjustments for errors are made by estimating the necessary change in the gap to hit the target. If the arrow falls short, the gap is lessened. The gap system merely provides a quick means for attaining some degree of proficiency with bare bow shooting at relatively short ranges and is not regarded as the ultimate in aiming procedure.

Sight Shooting. The mechanical device attached to the back or belly of the bow provides the most accurate means of aiming. A sight is relatively easy to use and allows for more exact corrections. Once the sight position for a given distance is known, a mark is made on the device itself or on the side of the bow. Prior knowledge of sight placement means that arrows will land in approximately the right spot at the very beginning of each practice session. Relatively minor adjustments for wind and weather conditions are made after a few shots. Moving the sight up and down changes the elevation of the bow arm. As the sight moves up, the bow arm is lowered. Adjustments for right-left errors (windage) are accomplished by moving the post in or out. If the arrow goes right (for a right-hand archer), the sight is moved or pushed in toward the bow. This causes the bow arm to move so that the arrow comes more in line with the center of the target. The sight is always moved in the direction of the error. If the arrow flies high and left, the sight is moved up and out. If the arrow is low and right, the sight is moved down and in.

On occasion, difficulty in using the sight is experienced. People are generally one-sided; that is, if they right-handed, they are also right-footed and aim with the right eye. People who are right-handed generally use the right eye for determining direction, the other eye provides distance depth perception. In some cases the dominant eye is not on the same side as the shooting hand; this can be bothersome in learning to use a sight. Check for eye dominance by pointing the index finger of the dominant hand directly at the center of a distant spot while both eyes are open. Cover the eye on the non-dominant side (left eye if left-handed) and then the other eye. If the eye that is used for determining direction is on the same side as the dominant hand, the finger will continue to point at the spot when this eye is exposed, and appear to jump to the side when the eye is covered. Any movement of the finger indicates that the eye is not functioning when focusing for direction. It is possible for a person with confused dominance to learn to shoot with a sight once he is aware of the condition.

Release

The act of sending the arrow on its path to the target could be thought of as archery's "moment of truth." All the preparation has occurred, all that remains is to loose the string. Contraction of the upper back muscles must be maintained or the hand will *creep* forward before the release resulting in a low flying arrow. Proper tension without strain or rigidity depends upon the archer's ability to accomplish the prerequisite phases correctly and upon his ability to free his mind of all outside distractions. The release itself is accomplished by simply relaxing the fingers. As contact with the string is broken, the action of the back muscles causes the elbow of the drawing arm to move back as the shoulder blades come together. The arm

Figure 5.10   Release and follow through.

and shoulder moves back as a single unit so that the hand passes alongside the neck.

There is a tendency to grip the bow as the string fingers relax. Every effort should be made to see that this does not occur. Attempt to keep the bow at draw level, but avoid excessive tension. Allow the bow to move naturally; it will move very slightly down and to the side. Attention to the release is important since it is easy to introduce many errors at this particular moment. Most indoor archery ranges and some schools have specially constructed training bows. The training bow is made so that it can be safely drawn and released without an arrow. Practice with these devices helps develop kinesthetic awareness in executing a good relaxed release. If a training bow is not available, the release can be practiced by pointing the arrow toward a nearby spot on the ground, drawing back 5 or 6" and relaxing the hand. A good release has the hand move backward as the string moves forward.

Follow Through or Afterhold

If errors in parts of the form remain undetected, their existence may actually be encouraged by rehearsal during practice sessions. The follow through involves maintaining the body, arm, and head position assumed at release until the arrow lands. What the archer does after the arrow leaves the bow does not affect the flight of the projectile. Extension of the release posture helps to point up the mistakes in execution which occurred before the release. Position of the bow arm, hands, head, shoulders, etc., provides information to the performer about errors in other parts of his form. Characteristics of a proper afterhold include the following:

1. Body erect, shoulders down and back, not collapsed.
2. Head toward the target, eyes focused on the objective.
3. Bow arm in extended position, little evidence of movement.
4. Fingers holding the bow are relaxed; no appreciable grasping has occurred.
5. String hand passed back along the side of the neck, fingers relaxed, free of tension.

Retrieving

Once the arrows are shot (hopefully into the intended target) all that remains is to collect them. Arrows impaled in a target butt are withdrawn by placing one hand on the face of the target close to the point of entry. The other hand grasps the shaft, not the fletching, near the pile. The arrow is withdrawn by twisting the shaft and pulling out at the angle of entry. Soft spots in some targets allow arrows to penetrate so that the fletching is fully or partly incorporated in the packing. Embedded arrows are retrieved with minor damage to the feathers by pulling them completely through the back side of the target. Ground arrows are collected in much the same manner as those hitting a target. If the fletching is free of entanglement the arrow is removed nock first. To retrieve buried arrows, the pile is located and the arrow pulled forward through the clutter until it is free. Special care should be exercised when securing glass and aluminum shafted arrows. Glass shafts can be broken when stepped on and aluminum shafts are bent if pressure is incorrectly applied during removal.

ANALYSIS OF PERFORMANCE

The objective of the shooting act is to have the arrows reach the intended target. Certain errors seem to occur regularly when shooting is first started. Generally speaking, these can be classified according to the hit (or miss) on the target. More than one factor can effect accuracy, and one error may cancel the effect of another. Observation by another person (instructor or student coach) is helpful in analyzing archery form. Faults are often very subtle or occur quickly so the observer must be aware of what to look for. The charts which follow indicate some of the more common shooting problems and provide information for correcting the difficulty.

TABLE 1

ANALYSIS OF THE FUNDAMENTALS

DIFFICULTY	PROBABLE CAUSE	SUGGESTED CORRECTION
INCORRECT HEAD POSITION – TILTED OR FORWARD	Face not turned directly toward target	Assume stance, looking straight ahead, then turn face toward target, keep head in this position throughout execution.
ARROW FALLS AWAY FROM BOW	Fingers used to draw the string instead of acting merely as hooks	Have elbow back at beginning; use back muscles to draw; practice partial draw, checking finger and hand position. Hand flattens as soon as elbow begins to move back if used properly.
	Pinching nock of arrow between index and middle finger	Finger should contact arrow nock lightly, no pressure. Place emphasis on drawing the string back, not the arrow. Try letting the fingers roll or twist the string during the draw, helps keep the arrow into the bow.
TOO MUCH EXTENSION OR STRAIGHTNESS OF BOW ARM	Arrow too long	Use shorter arrow but be careful to avoid an overdraw.
	Excessive pressure in pushing bow out	Place emphasis on draw not on pushing bow away.
GRASPING OR SQUEEZING BOW	Using muscles of bow hand to grip	Work for relaxed wrist and hand. Have only index finger and thumb around grip, exert very slight pressure. Practice string release with bow hand, work for relaxed wrist and hand as string leaves fingers.
FAILURE TO HOLD ANCHOR LONG ENOUGH	Bow too heavy	Use a lighter bow until sufficient strength is developed.
	Tendency to "snap shoot" or shoot too rapidly	Draw and hold anchor position for several seconds before releasing. Practice draw, hold, while aiming at a mirror or some object that has value to you. (Not a person, if you please.)

TABLE 1 (Continued)

DIFFICULTY	PROBABLE CAUSE	SUGGESTED CORRECTION
HUNCHED BOW SHOULDER	Bow too strong	Use lightest bow possible. Check arrow length, a shorter one may be needed. Practice fundamentals. Concentrate on keeping forward shoulder down and back. Experiment with open stance. (Forces shoulder down when aiming.)
AIMING WITH EYE ON THE BOW ARM SIDE	Inability to close the nonsighting eye	Practice winking the eye to strengthen muscles of the eye lid.
	Sighting with the eye on the non-dominant side	Check for dominant eye. Keep non-dominant eye closed when aiming.
HITTING ELBOW OF BOW ARM AT RELEASE	Arm hyperextended	Rotate elbow down and out in such a way that if flexion were to occur, the bow would swing into body (chest). Practice correct position mimetically or with a training bow until position becomes easy to assume.
	Attempting to draw an arrow that is too long	Check for correct arrow length, use those closest to the exact measurement.
BOW STRING REPEATEDLY HITS WRIST	Fistmele too short	Check correct bracing height; shorten string by twisting.
BRUISE OR CUTS ON TOP PART OF BOW HAND OR UPPER FINGER	Finger or hand held so that arrow touches it when leaving bow	Check hand position, use bow with an arrow rest if possible.
	Rough feathers; glue deposits usually at base of cock feather.	Sand area and wax.

TABLE 2

ANALYSIS OF DIRECTIONAL ERRORS

ARROW PLACEMENT	PROBABLE CAUSE	SUGGESTED CORRECTIONS
ARROWS SCATTERED; NO CONSISTENT PATTERN OR GROUPING	Faulty arrows — shaft bent or warped, vanes uneven or damaged	Check arrows; replace those damaged or bent.
	Arrows not matched properly	Use matched set if possible.
	Inconsistent form	Review and practice fundamentals.
	Inability to hold a stable position	Use a lighter bow; exercise to increase muscular strength.
	Arrow releases before proper aim has been accomplished.	Practice draw and hold.
ARROWS FLY HIGH OR OVER THE TARGET (12 O'CLOCK)	GENERAL: Sight too low; point of aim too close to target; gap too small	Move sight up; move aiming point closer to shooting line; increase size of gap.
	"Peeking" or looking up at release	Concentrate on target; hold head steady until arrow hits.
	Body "recoils" (moves back) at release	Hold body position steady until arrow hits.
	Heavier bow or different arrows than those normally used	Use same equipment each day of shooting or allow for adjustment when changing tackle.
	GRIP AND BOW ARM: Bow arm moves up or straightens at release	Work on holding proper bow arm position.
	Forefinger lifted causing arrow to be raised above plate or rest	Check grip; correct finger position.
	STRING ARM AND HAND: Arrow nocked too low	Make adjustment and mark proper nocking point.
	String pulled with less than three fingers; third finger allowed to slip off first	Place three fingers on string properly; work for complete relaxation of hand at release; practice partial draw and release into ground.

TABLE 2 (Continued)

ARROW PLACEMENT	PROBABLE CAUSE	SUGGESTED CORRECTIONS
	Lower jaw dropped (mouth opened); anchor lower than normal	Keep mouth in original position; use consistent anchor.
	"Jerking" (backward movement of hand before release)	Hold anchor position, work for relaxed finger release.
	Bow overdrawn	Use same anchor for each shot; check bow arm and shoulder position.
ARROWS FLY LOW OR FALL SHORT OF THE TARGET (6 O'CLOCK)	GENERAL: Sight too low; spot too close to archer; gap too large	Adjust sight (move down); select spot closer to target; shorten gap.
	Arrow released before full draw or before sight is properly aligned	Come to full draw and hold until properly "sighted in." Use a draw check device on the bow.
	Leaning or moving upper body forward at release	Maintain erect posture.
	Bow understrung	Check and correct fistmele.
	Insufficient bow power	Use heavier bow or move to a low anchor.
	Failure to compensate for a "headwind"	Make sight adjustments to allow for wind conditions.
	GRIP AND BOW ARM: Bow arm drops or collapses at release	Hold follow through, try to maintain elevation of bow arm without increasing tension.
	Bow arm fatigued, tends to "give."	Do not hold anchor and aim position so long that muscles tire; work to strengthen drawing muscles.
	Grip too low on bow	Put bow hand nearer top edge of grip.
	STRING ARM AND HAND: "Creeping" (arrow moves forward before release)	Keep anchor firm; work to strengthen drawing muscles.
	Draw elbow lowered on release	Make sure elbow moves directly back; keep it slightly above the shoulder when drawing.

TABLE 2 (Continued)

ARROW PLACEMENT	PROBABLE CAUSE	SUGGESTED CORRECTIONS
	Arrow nocked too high	Put a nocking point on the string 1/8" to 1/4" above the 90° angle formed by the arrow and the string; nock the arrow below this point.
ARROWS GO LEFT (9 O'CLOCK FOR RIGHT-HANDED SHOOTER)	GENERAL: Right-handed shooter (with dominant right eye) using left eye for aiming. (Arrows travel extremely left.)	Close or cover left eye, practice using right eye to aim.
	Aiming to the left of the bow string (arrows travel slightly left)	Head should be held so that the line of vision is slightly to the right of the string and the left of bow or directly through the string; the string is lined up with the left side of the bow so that there is no space visible; check string alignment on bow.
	Arrows too stiffly spined for bow (arrows slightly left)	Match bow and arrows; use heavier bow with same arrows; change arrows to more flexible ones for use with same bow.
	Failure to compensate for wind blowing to the left	Make windage adjustments for conditions. (Sight moves out or to left for right-handed shooter.)
	GRIP AND BOW ARM: Bow canted, upper limb tilted to the left	Have bow perpendicular, check with horizon; check pressure of bow grip; check head position, face directly toward target.
	Bow gripped too tightly, especially fingers on right side of bow	Place only thumb and forefinger around bow; put pressure into the belly of the bow; have bow contact heel of hand throughout.
	Flinching of the bow arm	Wear arm guard for protection and to prevent injury.
	Bow arm thrown to left at release	Hold follow through; work for relaxed bow arm; bow will move very slightly to side and down naturally.
	Wrist hyperextended; string to right of left edge of bow at full draw	Move wrist in line directly behind hand; check sight line through string and left side of bow.
	String hits arm or clothing	Wear appropriate clothing; remove jewelry or objects on left side of body; have shoulder go down and back in the draw.
	STRING ARM AND HAND: Not enough fingers on string; string held too close to tips	Three fingers should be used as hooks on the string; move string closer to first joint or use "deep hook."

TABLE 2 (Continued)

ARROW PLACEMENT	PROBABLE CAUSE	SUGGESTED CORRECTIONS
	"Plucking" — hand moves away from face sideways at release	Hand and arm should move back along the side of the neck. Practice release; keep string in firm contact until release.
	Arrow squeezed	Avoid putting pressure on arrow nock; string fingers only hooks; use back and upper arm muscles for draw.
	Anchor away from the side of the face	Use a solid anchor with consistent points of contact on the face; practice mimetics of shooting.
ARROWS TRAVEL RIGHT FOR RIGHT-HANDED ARCHER (3 O'CLOCK)	GENERAL: Stance closed, left foot not in line with or drawn back from right foot	Check foot position; be sure string is correctly aligned with side of bow at full draw.
	Arrows too flexible, weakly spined (go slightly right)	Match bow and arrows; use stiffer arrow with same bow; use same arrows with lighter bow.
	Aiming with left eye (which is dominant) when shooting right-handed	Learn to shoot left-handed if it is discovered early that left eye is dominant eye; point of aim or place where sight is held must be aligned left of intended target if right-handed shooting continues.
	Upper limb canted or tilted right	Bow should be perpendicular; check grip; put pressure into belly of the bow; check head position for tilting.
	No allowance for wind blowing to right	Move stance and adjust aim to compensate for wind conditions (sight moves right, closer to bow), may be necessary to select an object to left of target to aim at if wind deflection is severe.
	Feathers on arrow too large	Feathers should be trimmed to size to match weight of arrow shaft.
	GRIP AND BOW ARM: Bow hand and arm thrown to right at release	Work for controlled relaxation of left wrist at release; check left wrist for flexion; use back muscles for draw; check bow shoulder position (a hunched shoulder can contribute to the arm moving forward and to the right).
	Bow arm collapses to right across body on release	Maintain elevation of bow arm.
	Gripping wrist flexed	Move wrist to position directly behind hand.
	STRING HAND AND ARM: String to left of left side of bow at full draw	Check line of vision through string and edge of bow; no space or gap showing.
	String jerked to left on or just before release	Hold anchor firm until release; work for relaxed finger release so hand and arm move straight back.

BASIC SAFETY CONSIDERATIONS

Archery is not dangerous; people are! The bow and arrow is a weapon and should be considered as such. Weapons possess the potential to seriously injure or permanently maim if used without discretion.

General Safety

1. Develop safety consciousness.
2. Shoot only in appropriate areas.
3. Allow sufficient space between archers.
4. Nock arrows only when the shooting area is clear.
5. Don't draw the bow back with an arrow unless you are going to shoot.
6. Always have a definite target at which to aim. Shooting arrows straight into the air is dangerous and rather senseless.
7. Avoid wearing clothes or jewelry that may catch the bow string.
8. Practice courtesy and consideration of others.

Safety in the Technique of Shooting

1. Avoid a stiff straight bow arm. The arm should be rotated out. When the arm is in correct position, the bow will move directly toward the body when the elbow is flexed.
2. The index finger of the bow hand should be around the handle, not alongside the arrow on release.
3. Always use an arm guard and finger protection.
4. Keep the bow arm in proper position to avoid an overdraw.
5. Never point an arrow at anyone, whether the bow is drawn or not.
6. Step back from the shooting line until everyone has finished shooting.

Safety on the Range and at the Target

1. Use a common shooting line. Move the targets to allow archers to practice at different distances at the same time.
2. Check to see that the targets are firmly anchored.
3. Check for rocks in the shooting area.
4. Stand away from the person withdrawing arrows from the target.
5. When shooting in a group, retrieving and shooting should not be carried on at the same time. Even when targets are far apart there is danger of an arrow glancing to the right or left and hitting someone who is retrieving.

Safety with the Bow

1. Never release the string without an arrow.
2. Check the bow string regularly for frayed string or serving.
3. Bows which have been stored for some time of that have been in the cold should be warmed up gradually.
4. Check the bow for cracks or splintering.
5. Check the fistmele of the bow.
6. Do not use a bow that is too heavy for you.
7. When bracing the bow, follow several precautions:
   Make sure the lower end is properly secured at the foot.
   Apply pressure equally at three points.
   Be careful not to get the fingers caught under the string.
   Be sure both ends of the string are entirely in the nock.
8. Do not overdraw as the bow may break.

Safety with Arrows

1. Avoid using cracked or split arrows; check arrows after each end.

2. Take care in drawing accurately; the arrow may go wild or into the hand if overdrawn.
3. Be sure the arrow is of sufficient length.
4. If the arrow slips when drawing, start over; don't push up with the finger and keep drawing or the arrow may be released too soon and fly wild.
5. Avoid pinching the nock at release.

SUGGESTED TASKS FOR THE STUDENT

(NOTE: These tasks should be performed in a safe manner. It would be wise to secure the instructor's permission before attempting them.)

1. Practice putting on the arm guard and finger tab or glove. Check with the instructor to see if you are doing it properly.
2. Brace the bow several times using both the procedures described. "Talk" someone else through the stringing process.
3. After you have had some shooting experience, experiment with the stance and weight distribution. Describe any differences in results to a fellow student.
4. Draw a bow with a standard handle and one which has a contoured grip. Describe any differences you experience.
5. Shoot arrows nocked in the manner indicated in the text and also with the cock feather turned toward the bow. Check for differences in flight and for damage to the fletching.
6. Experiment with the shallow hook and the deep hook. Determine which technique is most comfortable and results in the smoothest release.
7. Draw a diagram of the flight of your arrows to a target from a distance of 40 yards using a high anchor position. Draw a diagram of the arrow's trajectory using a low anchor for the same distance. What conclusion can you draw from your pictures?

8. Construct a homemade bow sight or point of aim device.
9. Construct a chart or checklist for use in analyzing shooting form. Using your checklist, observe a fellow student's performance; locate any difficulties and write out suggestions for improvement.
10. Have someone take slow motion pictures of your shooting form. Analyze your shooting form and write out a plan for self-improvement.

Archery
Sports
and
Games

Fundamental archery skills can be applied in a variety of sports and games. Target archery, field archery, indoor archery, clout shooting, and flight shooting are conducted as athletic contests. The National Archery Association (NAA) provides information on the layout of shooting ranges, tournament rules, championship rounds, clout, team, cross bow, and flight shooting. Field archery has a separate governing body. Hunting and fishing are mainly recreational activities. A number of games and novelty shoots have been developed. Some of these games simulate conditions encountered in hunting, others are variations of existing games. All are fun and provide an opportunity to improve skill in shooting.

The emphasis in this chapter is on target archery since this is the form of the sport most often taught in schools and colleges. Once the basics of shooting are mastered, the opportunity for their application is limited only by the imagination and interest of the shooter.

CONVENTIONAL TARGET ARCHERY

Target archery is conducted on a shooting range where the participants send arrows into a standard five-color target. Each archer shoots a given number of arrows from certain designated distances according to a set procedure. Knowledge of terminology, scoring, rules, and tournament procedure are necessary for participation. Each sport has its own unique vocabulary. Similar terms may be used in more than one form of the sport but may have different meanings. The list below pertains to conventional target archery.

Terminology

END   Six arrows shot consecutively or in two groups of three.

FIELD CAPTAIN OR LADY PARAMOUNT   The presiding official in charge of a tournament.

HIT   An arrow that lands within the scoring area on the target.

PENETRATION   An arrow imbedded in the target so that it is not visible on the face or one that passes completely through the target.

PETTICOAT   The edge of the target beyond the outside ring. An arrow striking this area does not score or count as a hit.

RANGE   The distance to be shot; the shooting area; an indoor or outdoor archery ground.

REBOUND   An arrow that bounces off the scoring area of the target.

ROUND   A term used to describe a given number of arrows or ends shot at a designated distance or distances.

TARGET CAPTAIN   The archer in charge of each target.

Scoring

All target archery rounds are shot at a regulation 48" target face unless otherwise specified. Target faces are divided into five concentric rings and scored from the center outward. The middle or gold counts nine points, the red seven points, the blue five points, the black three points and the white one point. For international competition, each of the rings is divided in half and the top score is ten so that the gold counts ten and nine; the red eight and seven; the blue six and five; the black four and three; and the white two and one.

An arrow cutting the fine line dividing two colors is scored as the higher value. Rebounds or penetrations, if witnessed, receive seven points if the distance is 60 yards or less or five points if the distance is greater than 60 yards. Arrows are pulled from the scoring face by the target captain and recorded on the score sheet with the highest numerical value first and the lowest last. A sample score card for a Columbia Round is shown in Fig. 6.1. In the American Round the archers each shoot 30 arrows at 60, 50, and 40 yards. In the Columbia Round the archers each shoot 24 arrows at 50, 40, and 30 yards.

Tournament Shooting

In tournament shooting, the archers are usually assigned to targets in the order in which they register. After the first round or the first half of a single round, the archers are reassigned so

Figure 6.1   Score card.

ARCHERY SCORE							
Name _J. SMITH_							
Date _MAY 3_				196_9_		Hits	Score
Yds.	7	5	3	1	0	0	4	16
	9	7	7	5	1	0	5	29
50	7	7	5	3	3	1	6	26
	9	9	7	3	0	0	4	28
Percentage					Total	19	99
Yds.	7	5	1	0	0	0	3	13
	9	5	3	3	1	0	5	21
40	9	9	7	5	5	3	6	38
	9	9	7	7	3	1	6	36
Percentage					Total	20	108
Yds.	7	7	7	5	1	1	6	28
	9	7	7	5	3	3	6	34
30	9	9	9	9	5	1	6	42
	9	9	9	7	7	5	6	46
Percentage					Total	24	150
Grand Total					Total	63	357
TEAM TOTAL							

that those with the highest scores are placed on the first target, next highest on the second target and so on. No more than five and preferably only four people are assigned to a given target. Each of the archers has specific duties and responsibilities in a tournament.

Target Captain. The first person listed on the score sheet acts as the target captain. Before the arrows are withdrawn and scored, he examines the target to determine whether there are any questionable arrows. If he cannot make a decision on an arrow, the field captain or lady paramount is called. Once the face of the target has been checked, the target captain pulls the arrows for each archer separately, calling tne values as he does so.

Scorers. The second two people on the score sheet are designated as the scorers. They record the scores as called by the target captain and add the totals. Two scorers are used to avoid mistakes and they check with one another after each end and each distance round.

Retrievers. The remaining shooters are assigned to retrieve all arrows which miss the target.

Field Captain or Lady Paramount. The presiding official in a tournament signals the start and finish of each end of shooting. Any problems or scoring decisions that cannot be resolved by the target captain are referred to this official.

Split ends are customary in most large tournaments. A split end consists of the first two archers shooting three arrows each, followed by the second group of two or three archers shooting the same. The first two shooters then shoot their last three arrows, followed by the second group.

Rules for Competition and Safety

Rules are necessary for any sport. Some safety rules have already been presented in a previous chapter and these should be reviewed. Here are a summary of competition rules and some additional safety procedures:

1. All archers shoot from and straddle a common shooting line.
2. Arrows are nocked after the signal to shoot is given.
3. Only six arrows may be legally shot; if more than six are shot, only the lowest six are scored.

4. Arrows are considered shot if they fall from the bow and cannot be reached with the aid of the bow while standing on the shooting line.
5. After shooting an end, step back from the shooting line until the signal to retrieve is given. Courtesy dictates that you remain on the line until others on your target have completed their end.
6. Arrows must remain in the target until withdrawn by the target captain.
7. Retrieve arrows only on the appropriate signal.
8. The longest distance round is shot first, the second longest next, and so forth.
9. If scores are tied, the highest score at the longest distance determines the winner.
10. No practice is permitted between the distances which constitute a round once the tournament is underway. All practice ends must be shot prior to the start of shooting for score.
11. Arrows must have distinctive markings or crests so that the individual archer's arrows are easily identified.
12. All bows, except a cross bow, are legal for tournament competition.
13. Only a legal sight attached to the bow may be used.
14. Point of aim markers may not be placed more than 6" above the ground.
15. Scores are recorded from high to low. Misses or arrows landing outside the scoring face are indicated with a zero.

Common Tournament Rounds

The National Archery Association classifies archers by age and sex for purposes of competition. Beginners are eleven years and younger, juniors are twelve to fourteen, intermediates, fifteen to seventeen, and adults, eighteen and older. Competitive rounds are available for each classification. The chart which follows summarizes some of the more common rounds of interest to students at the college level.

TABLE 3
COMMON TARGET ROUNDS

ROUND	ENDS	DISTANCE	ARROWS (6 PER END)	TOTAL	MAXIMUM SCORE	COMMONLY SHOT BY
AMERICAN	5	60 Yards	30	90 Arrows	810	Men, Women,
	5	50 Yards	30	15 Ends		Intermediates
	5	40 Yards	30			
COLUMBIA	4	50 Yards	24	72 Arrows	748	Women; Inter-
	4	40 Yards	24	12 Ends		mediate and
	4	30 Yards	24			Junior Girls;
						High School
						and College
						Students
HEREFORD	12	80 Yards	72	144 Arrows	1296	Women;
	8	60 Yards	48	12 Ends		Intermediate
	4	50 Yards	24			Boys
YORK	12	100 Yards	72	144 Arrows	1296	Men
	8	80 Yards	48	12 Ends		
	4	60 Yards	24			
WOMEN'S	5	60 Yards	30	120 Arrows	1080	Women
METROPOLITAN	5	50 Yards	30	20 Ends		
	5	40 Yards	30			
	5	30 Yards	30			
MEN'S	5	100 Yards	30	150 Arrows	1350	Men
METROPOLITAN	5	80 Yards	30	25 Ends		
	5	60 Yards	30			
	5	50 Yards	30			
	5	40 Yards	30			
SCHOLASTIC	4	40 Yards	24	48 Arrows	432	College and
	4	30 Yards	24	8 Ends		Senior High
						Students

(NOTE: All rounds shot on regulation 48″, four-color target and scored 9—7—5—3—1.)

Operation Archery Round

The operation archery round is a combination of one of the newer target rounds and a modification of a field archery round.

Part I   Modified Chicago Round (Score 5 – 4 – 3 – 2 – 1).   6 ends (5 arrows each end) at 20 yards; 36″ face.

Part II Modified Flint Round (Score 5 − 3).

Station 1	4 Arrows	at	17 Yards	18-inch face
Station 2	4 Arrows	at	20 Feet	12-inch face
Station 3	4 Arrows	at	20 Yards	18-inch face
Station 4	4 Arrows	at	14 Yards	12-inch face
Station 5	4 Arrows	at	15 Yards	18-inch face
Station 6	4 Arrows	at	10 Yards	12-inch face
Station 7	1 Arrow	at	12 Yards	18-inch face
	1 Arrow	at	17 Yards	18-inch face
	1 Arrow	at	15 Yards	18-inch face
	1 Arrow	at	14 Yards	18-inch face
	1 Arrow	at	10 Yards	18-inch face
	1 Arrow	at	20 Feet	18-inch face

PERFECT SCORE FOR ROUND: Modified Chicago 150

Modified Flint 150

300

Team Competition

Many schools and clubs have team competitions. A team usually consists of four members, but the number can vary. In competition, any number may form a team provided that the teams competing have an equal number of participants. Clubs often shoot against one another and average the scores of all shooters to determine the winner. Team rounds suggested by the NAA consist of 96 arrows at 60 yards for men and 96 arrows at 50 yards for women.

The national Collegiate Archery Coaches Association (sanctioned by NAA) promotes competition at the college and university level. Meets are conducted on a shoulder-to-shoulder basis as well as by mail or telegram. In shoulder-to-shoulder competition, all shooters are present on the same range. In mail or telegraphic shoots, the archers compete on their home range and the scores are forwarded to the tournament chairman or host school. The types of rounds shot vary with the tournament. The National Intercollegiate Archery Championship tournament requires a Double Columbia Round (two complete

Columbia Rounds) for women and a Double American Round for men. The NCACA National Intercollegiate Championships for men, women, and teams are decided at this tournament.

The NCACA, which governs college and university competition, was formed in 1962. The group has worked hard to promote the sport of archery and make it part of the general collegiate athletic program. Hopefully, competition at the college level will provide more and better qualified archers for future Olympic teams.

Modern Target Archery

The upswing of interest in archery as a competitive sport has led to the development of a number of variations in conventional target archery. Many new competitive rounds have been initiated, designed to appeal to archers of all levels of ability; many can be used equally well indoors and outdoors. Some of the newer rounds are adaptations or modifications of field archery rounds, and require the archer to shoot from several distances at targets varying in size and design. Others use the more conventional five-color target but the size is smaller and scoring starts with a high of five points and goes to a low of one point. All of the rounds are based on a perfect score of 300 and only five arrows constitute an end. The perfect 300 resembles the score associated with bowling. The idea of one top score for several different rounds is useful since it enables people to interpret the score in relation to a set standard. A number of the newer rounds are outlined in the following chart.

INDOOR ARCHERY LANES

Indoor archery lanes are a relatively new innovation. The advent of the automated target has been a boon to the serious archer and has extended the opportunity for participation to many others. Archery has traditionally been an outdoors sport. This meant that the shooter had to have sufficient free time during daylight hours to practice and compete. Indoor archery

TABLE 4

NEWER COMPETITIVE ROUNDS

ROUND	ENDS	DISTANCE	ARROWS (5 PER END)	TOTAL	SCORING & TARGET	MAXIMUM SCORE
SCOT	12	20 Yards	60	60 Arrows 12 Ends	5-4-3-2-1 25" Black and Gray	300
PROFESSIONAL	12	20 Yards	60	60 Arrows 12 Ends	5-4-3-2-1 16" Black, P.A.A.	300
SECTIONAL	12	30 Yards	60	60 Arrows 12 Ends	5-4-3-2-1 36" Four Color	300
CONFERENCE	4 4 4	50 Yards 40 Yards 30 Yards	20 20 20	60 Arrows 12 Ends	5-4-3-2-1 48" Four Color	300
GRAND AMERICAN	4 4 4	60 Yards 50 Yards 40 Yards	20 20 20	60 Arrows 12 Ends	5-4-3-2-1 48" Four Color	300

is now available at all hours, and even seasonal changes do not effect its operation.

Archery lanes are operated in a manner similar to bowling lanes. The house has the necessary equipment available, and the archer pays an hourly rate for use of the facilities. Most operators provide an instructor to help beginners and coach more advanced performers. The archer shoots at a target which moves automatically to any distance he selects. Arrows are retrieved by pressing a button on the console causing the target to move up to the shooting line. Once the target has reached the shooter, he scores his hits and removes his arrows. Most archery centers have leagues which operate during the evening hours. The leagues are often handicapped, and it is not unusual to have teams composed of all men, all women, and couples shooting against one another. Archery enthusiasts are hopeful that their sport will become as popular as bowling and golf and feel that the automated lanes will foster the growth and development of this sport.

FIELD ARCHERY

Interest in field archery has grown tremendously since the first official tournament held in 1946. The National Field Archery Association (NFAA) is the governing organization, providing information on course construction, rules interpretation, formation of clubs, and sponsorship of tournaments. Field archery tournaments are conducted in both freestyle (sight shooters) and bare bow (instinctive shooters) classifications.

The main difference between target and field archery is the structure of the shooting range. Both sports involve shooting at stationary targets, but in field archery the range is larger and involves a variety of terrain. The archer moves from one shooting station to another, often through woods and brush, and shoots at special field faces. The distances shot differ at each target, and some stations require shots from more than one position   The size of the target faces used range from 12 to 24" depending on the distance shot.   An end in field consists of four arrows. The standard field target face has two concentric circles with an aiming spot in the center. A hit in the inner circle scores five points and one in the outer circle, three. This exciting and challenging sport places many demands on the archer; it is easy to see why this form of archery has become so popular ove; the last several years.

CLOUT SHOOTING

Clout shooting is a form of competition sanctioned by the NAA but it is also engaged in as a "fun" activity. Distances used in clout rounds vary with the archer's shooting classification. Ladies shoot from a distance of 120 or 140 yards. Men are placed 180 yards from the target. The clout target resembles that used for conventional target archery except that it is 48' in diameter and laid out on the ground. The archer sends his arrows high into the air toward a flag marking the center of the target. A clout round consists of 36 arrows (6 ends) and is scored in the same manner as the conventional five-color target.

FLIGHT SHOOTING

The basic idea in flight shooting is to send an arrow the maximum distance possible. Competitors are restricted to certain categories authorized by the NAA. Each division is further classified by weight and type of bow. Each classification has an unlimited weight competition and a foot bow competition. The foot bow is a bow with an extremely heavy draw weight that is drawn with both hands while braced against the archer's feet. Flight shooting has limited appeal, but its enthusiasts are dedicated. It is not unusual for an adherent of the sport to spend months designing and constructing a flight shooting bow in an effort to make that one perfect shot.

HUNTING

Hunting is different from competitive archery in many ways. Every hunter must be familiar with the basics of shooting but must also be able to adjust his tackle and technique for different game. Hunting arrows are designed to accommodate a larger, heavier point and, usually, longer feathers. Bow hunting is a very specialized form of archery and requires much more than the ability to handle a bow and arrow competently. The hunter must employ other skills and be familiar with the habits of the game he is stalking. Students concerned with the hunting aspect of archery are urged to master the fundamentals of shooting and practice with the equipment they intend to use. Although there are several informative books on the sport of bow hunting, the best means to learn is to participate with an experienced bow hunter.

GAMES AND NOVELTY SHOOTS

Archery games can be played on the range, in the backyard, or almost any convenient, safe area. The games and novelty shoots included here present unique challenges to the archer. All can be a source of fun and enjoyment while helping to perfect shooting skill.

Archery Golf. Archery golf is played on a regulation golf course or on any large outdoor area. The rules are basically the same as those used for playing golf. The "cup" consists of a ball placed on a stand which the archer must hit to complete the hole. When the game is played on a regulation course, a par of one stroke less than that designated for the golfer is used. Archery golf combines elements of the clout and target techniques and requires good depth perception and accuracy.

Roving Archery. Archers move about an area in groups of three or four and pick targets at random. The target might be a piece of paper, a bush, a clump of grass, or the like. Each archer shoots one arrow at the target selected. The shooter who hits the target or comes closest receives a point and has the privilege of determining the next target.

Wand Shooting. The target is made of soft wood, 2" wide and 6' high. Women shoot 36 arrows at 60 yards. Men shoot 36 arrows at 100 yards. The wood is usually placed over a butt so that misses are stopped immediately. Arrows rebounding from the wand are scored as hits. Wand shooting is a very old archery game and was played in England as early as the sixteenth century.

Pope Young Round. This is a round for speed and accuracy. Six shooting stations are set up. Six targets are arranged from 20 to 80 yards. Six ends constitute a round. Six arrows are shot from one station in 45 seconds. Each arrow is shot at a different target. After each end is scored, the archers move to another station in a rotating order. One point is scored per hit. Animal faces may be used as targets. (**Note: This round should only be used by archers who have had experience and who shoot with sights or instinctively.**)

Tic Tac Toe. Nine balloons are arranged on the target in lines of three across and three down. Archers on each target form a file. At the signal to shoot, the first archer shoots one arrow and goes to the end of the line. Each succeeding player repeats the action. The first team to break three balloons in any straight line wins. The distance from the target can vary but 20 yards seems to offer sufficient challenge for the average person. As a point of safety, no one is allowed to take an arrow from the quiver until on the shooting line.

Still-Hunting the Buck. A burlap deer is constructed with 2 ovals marking its vitals, the heart being inside the larger oval. One player hides the deer, leaving a trail of kernels of corn dropping one every yard. After ten minutes the hunters surge forth. The first to sight the deer calls, "Deer." He shoots from that point. If he misses in three tries, the others shoot one arrow each. If all miss, they take five steps and shoot again. This continues until they are 10 yards from the deer, or until it is hit; in which case further shooting is done from the spot where the hit was made. A shot in the heart scores ten and ends the hunt. A shot in the large oval scores five. A hit outside the oval scores two. If all shoot 10 yards from the deer without a hit, the hider scores 25 and the deer is hidden again. The hunter with the highest score wins.

Bow Bird Shooting. Flu-flu arrows and bow bird targets are needed for this game. Both items can be purchased commercially. If flu-flu arrows are not available reasonably satisfactory ones can be made by using the "feathers" of plastic badminton birds. The heads of the plastic shuttlecocks often wear out and the entire bird is discarded. To convert a regular target arrow into a flu-flu arrow, remove the plastic part of the shuttlecock and cut lines in the base so that it will slide up the shaft of the arrow close to the feathers. A small game blunt is attached to the pile end of the arrow for balance. These arrows will not fly as true as those that are specially made, but prove quite satisfactory for this game. Bow bird targets can be constructed by taping together circular disks cut out of heavy cardboard. Plastic "flying saucers" can also be used for targets.

The game is usually played as a team activity. The archers are lined up behind one another with a thrower to one side (hidden from view if possible). A member of each team steps to the line. When each has his arrow nocked, the range captain calls, "Pull." The thrower can throw the bird at any time within 20 seconds after the call and at any angle or elevation. Each team member gets at least three shots. Hits count for score and the high team total wins. A target distance of about 10 yards in front of the shooting line seems to be satisfactory for this game.

Other Games. There are a great many other games that can be played with the use of the bow and arrow. Archers can shoot at targets from different positions such as kneeling, standing on one leg, or left-handed. The object of Archery Monopoly is to get all arrows in one color and if successful, the shooter gets to keep all of the arrows in that color. The target can also be scored backwards so that the white ring is high and the gold ring low. Stuffed rabbit hunts, a number of balloon events and shoots that use specially constructed target faces are additional activities. The list is almost endless and a credit to the creativity of the archery enthusiast.

SUGGESTED TASKS FOR THE STUDENT

1. Determine the location of all archery clubs and ranges in the area surrounding your school and permanent residence.
2. Arrange to observe an archery tournament in progress. List the procedures you observe regarding safety, dress of the participants, the method of scoring, the duties of the archers, the general conduct of the participants, and so forth.
3. Visit an indoor archery lane if there is one in your area.
4. Determine how many schools and colleges in your vicinity have archery teams and the extent of their activity.
5. Indicate how you would go about finding information on rules, course layouts, and tournament procedure for the various competitive archery sports.
6. Make up a special archery round that is suitable for use at your institution.
7. Determine a means of establishing handicaps for equalizing competition among archers of varying levels of ability.
8. Make up a game or novelty shoot that can be played by members of your class.

Pointing Up
Progress

Earlier in this book, it was maintained that the learner must do his own learning. An instructor helps shorten the learning time by eliminating much of the trial and error, but it is still necessary to apply the instructor's suggestions to the performance. Archery activity provides immediate feedback information. Knowledge of results helps to point up progress and serves to reinforce learning. Quantitative archery scores provide information about level of ability and are a meaningful indication of learning. A systematic means of recording progress helps determine the exact amount of improvement and denotes areas in need of attention. Several means of analyzing and evaluating shooting ability are presented in this section. The list of suggested tasks for the student, included at the end of each of the preceding chapters, also contributes to evaluation and reinforcement of learning.

ANALYSIS OF FORM AND GENERAL KNOWLEDGE

Checklists and rating sheets are useful for self-appraisal as well as for evaluation by another person. The ratings effectively isolate individual difficulties and aid in determining the nature of the experiences necessary to remedy the problems.

Self-Checklist

Figure 7.1   Example of a self checklist.

DIRECTIONS: Place the dates you checked each item in the columns to the left. Enter the date you *know* you mastered each task in the right-hand column.

		TASK		COMMENTS
		1. Brace bow correctly		
		2. Nock arrow correctly		
		3. Grip in "V," wrist aligned		
		4. Hold bow arm in slightly flexed position with shoulder down		
		5. Draw with upper back, shoulder and upper arm muscles		
		6. Use three fingers as hooks on string		
		7. Use exactly same foot position and weight distribution		
		8. Draw to exactly the same anchor and distance		
		9. Hold long enough to aim		
		10. Follow through after release		
		11. Use a sight correctly		
		12. Keep a score sheet		
		13. Analyze form and correct for the errors		
		14. Group arrows on the target		
		15 Retrieve arrows correctly		

Rating Sheet

Figure 7.2 Archery rating sheet.

NAME:	DATE:	/ / / /	COMMENTS

STANCE
- Feet not placed consistently
- Weight uneven
- Body incorrectly aligned

NOCK
- Nocking point inconsistent
- Position of fingers incorrect

DRAW
- Pressure on arrow nock
- String fingers and arm used
- Bow wrist flexed or hyperextended
- Draw elbow below wrist of drawing hand
- Bow canted
- Bow elbow not rotated out
- Bow shoulder hunched
- Head moves or tilts
- Body moves

AIM ANCHOR
- Incorrect eye used
- Bow arm unsteady
- Anchor inconsistent
- No hold or aim apparent

RELEASE
- Body moves
- Bow arm moves
- String arm and hand moves incorrectly

HOLD No follow through

GROUPING WHILE RATED   RATED BY:

1   2   3   4

1.
2.
3.
4.

Photographs and Pictures. Many schools now own portable television taping machines. These can provide an immediate picture of the performance and are extremely beneficial in analyzing form. Graph-check photographs aid in analysis and furnish a permanent visual record of individual form. Moving pictures and still photographs also supply a means of checking technique and, if taken often enough, serve as a record of progress. For best results, pictures should be used in conjunction with the charts previously indicated.

SCORE AND ACCURACY ANALYSIS

Scores, plotted on a graph or compared with established standards, are another means of ascertaining individual development. The use of a card or form to locate hits on, or in the area of the target, helps in determining progress and points to areas in need of practice.

Accuracy Analysis Chart. The position of each arrow is marked with a dot for each end of shooting at each distance. If the cards are properly dated and filed, progress, or lack of it, is clearly evident. The record also helps to indicate the existence of a faulty arrow in the set. If arrows are numbered or individually identified in some manner, the code for the arrow is entered on the card in the appropriate space. Faulty or damaged arrows are easily located after a few ends.

Profile Chart. Profile charts, plotted on graph paper for selected rounds or distances, provide visual evidence of progress. The chart often has valleys and peaks, but improvement should be demonstrated over an extended period. Scores that dip

Figure 7.3 Example of a graph-check photograph. What suggestions can *you* make to improve the form?

below the average over several shooting sessions indicate the need to look for errors in form or other learning problems.

Percentiles. Most schools keep records of scores made by students in archery classes over a period of several years. Percentile tables are constructed and posted for reference. Individual progress and achievement is determined by checking personal scores against the chart. If the score falls at the sixtieth percentile, it means that the individual scored better than 60 per cent of the students who were enrolled in a similar class. Checking percentiles for each complete round or for each distance shot also provides a meaningful record of improvement. If at the beginning of the course scores are at the tenth percentile and halfway through have moved to the fortieth, the implication is clearly evident.

The American Association for Health, Physical Education, and Recreation recently published an *Archery Skills Test Manual*. The booklet contains percentiles for different age levels at distances of 10, 20, and 30 yards. If no other records are available, these may prove helpful as a guide in estimating ability. The library or the instructor should have a copy of this booklet.

Figure 7.4 Accuracy analysis chart.

ACCURACY ANALYSIS CHART

Name _____ Date _____ Card No. _____

Distance: _____   Suggested Corrections

Made by: _____

INDIVIDUAL PROGRAMS

Each learner learns at his own rate. This must be kept in mind as achievement is measured. Each person needs to establish his own goal and work out a plan for reaching it. The devices indicated above are helpful in implementing progress toward the objective, but the objective must clearly be the intent of the learner.

Programs can be quantitative (a score or number), or qualitative (how well), or both. One idea for designing an individual program at different levels is presented above. Each student is urged to think through all the tasks involved in learning to handle a bow and arrow competently, and to design his own program for accomplishing them.

Learning is a process as well as a product. The more you, the student, are involved in the learning process, the more meaningful and satisfying the experience becomes. The end product may be a certain skill level in shooting a bow and arrow, but in the process you may also discover a new image of yourself. *Archery is a means to an end — an end in itself.*

Figure 7.5   Example of individual program design-multi-level.

INDIVIDUAL PROGRAM NO. _____

Name _____

TASK: Shoot _____ arrows or _____ ends from a distance of _____ yards

LEVELS	DESCRIPTION	A	B	COMMENTS/REACTIONS
Level 1	$\frac{1}{2}$ of all arrows shot, each end, hit scoring area			
Level 2	All arrows shot, each end, hit scoring area			
Level 3	All arrows shot hit on or inside the blue ring			
Level 4	Score not less than _____ for each end shot with all arrows hitting within scoring area			

DIRECTIONS: In column A record the date you were <u>first</u> able to accomplish the task at the given level. In column B put the date you were able to accomplish the task on ___ consecutive days of shooting.

Suggested Readings

Ainsworth, Dorothy S. et. al., *Individual Sports for Women*. Philadelphia, Penn.: W. B. Saunders Company, 1955.

American Association for Health, Physical Education, and Recreation, *Archery Skills Test Manual*. Washington, D.C.: AAHPER, 1967.

Beisser, Arnold R., *The Madness in Sports*. New York, N.Y.: Appleton-Century-Crofts, 1967.

Burke, Edmund H., *Archery Handbook*. Greenwich, Conn.: Fawcett Publications, Inc., 1954.

_____, *Field and Target Archery*. Greenwich, Conn.: Fawcett Publications, Inc., 1961.

_____, *The History of Archery*. New York, N.Y.: William Morrow and Co., 1957.

Division for Girls' and Women's Sports, *Archery-Riding Guide*. Washington, D.C.: AAHPER.

Elmer, Robert P., *Target Archery*. New York, N.Y.: Alfred A. Knopf, Inc., 1946.

Forbes, Thomas A., *New Guide to Better Archery*. Harrisburg, Penn.: Stackpole Co., 1960.

Haugen, Arnold O. and Harlan G. Metcalf, *Field Archery and Bowhunting*. New York, N.Y.: Ronald Press Company, 1963.

Herrigel, Eugen, *Zen in the Art of Archery*. New York, N.Y.: McGraw-Hill, Inc., 1964.

Houghman, Paul C., *The Encyclopedia of Archery*. New York, N.Y.: A. S. Barnes and Co., 1957.

Jaeger, Eloise, *Archery Instructor's Guide*. Chicago, Ill.: The Athletic Institute, 1960.

Keaggy, David J., Sr., *Power Archery*. Riderwood, Md.: *Archery World Magazine*, 1964.

Love, Albert J., *Field Archery Technique*. Corpus Christie, Texas: Dotson Publishing Company, 1956.

McKinney, Wayne C., *Archery*. Dubuque, Iowa: William C. Brown Co., 1966.

Metheny, Eleanor, *Movement and Meaning*. New York, N.Y.: McGraw-Hill, Inc., 1968.

Miller, Myrtle K., *General Archery Safety Rules*. 67 Old Stone Church Road, Upper Saddle River, New Jersey.

_____, *Practical Aids for Archery Instructors*. 67 Old Stone Church Road, Upper Saddle River, New Jersey.

Mosston, Muska, *Teaching Physical Education*. Columbus, Ohio: Charles E. Merrill Co., 1966.

National Field Archery Assocation, *Archery*. P.O. Box H, Palm Springs, California.

Niemeyer, Roy K., *Beginning Archery*. Belmont, Calif.: Wadsworth Publishing Company, Inc., 1967.

Oxendine, Joseph B., *Psychology of Motor Learning*. New York, N.Y.: Appleton-Century-Crofts, 1968.

Pearson, Ben, *Archery for Everyone*. Pine Bluff, Arkansas: Ben Pearson, Inc.

Singer, Robert H., *Motor Learning and Human Performance*. New York, N.Y.: Macmillan Co., 1968.